T0198703

Parenting Kids With OCD

Parenting Kids With OCD

A Guide to Understanding and Supporting Your Child With Obsessive-Compulsive Disorder

Bonnie Zucker, Psy.D.

Routledge
Taylor & Francis Group

NEW YORK AND LONDON

Dedication

For Brian, Isaac, and Todd:

Your love is my home, and
Nothing is as pure and as perfect.
Thank you for your support, enthusiasm,
And the sweetness you bring to my life.

Library of Congress Cataloging-in-Publication Data

Names: Zucker, Bonnie, 1974- author.
Title: Parenting kids with OCD : a guide to understanding and supporting your
  child with obsessive-compulsive disorder / by Bonnie Zucker, Psy.D.
Description: Waco, Texas : Prufrock Press Inc., [2018] | Includes
  bibliographical references.
Identifiers: LCCN 2017032967 (print) | LCCN 2017038430 (ebook) | ISBN
9781618216663 (pbk.) Subjects: LCSH: Obsessive-compulsive disorder in
adolescence--Popular works.
  | Obsessive-compulsive disorder in children--Popular works. |
  Parenting--Popular works. | Parent and child--Popular works.
Classification: LCC RJ506.O25 (ebook) | LCC RJ506.O25 Z82 2018 (print) | DDC
  618.9285/227--dc23
LC record available at https://lccn.loc.gov/2017032967

First published in 2018 by Prufrock Press Inc.

Published in 2021 by Routledge
605 Third Avenue, New York, NY 10017
2 Park Square, Milton Park, Abingdon, Oxon OX14 4RN

Routledge is an imprint of the Taylor & Francis Group, an informa business

Copyright ©2018, Bonnie Zucker, Psy.D.

Cover and layout design by Raquel Trevino

ISBN: 9781618216663 (pbk)

DOI: 10.4324/9781003237044

Table of Contents

Acknowledgments

Many years ago, in graduate school, I read an article entitled "The Privilege of Being a Therapist." I grasped the concept, but at the time my excitement for the field of psychology and the work I couldn't wait to do overshadowed what would end up being the most meaningful part. It wasn't until I entered into private practice and had the daily firsthand experience of having children, teens, and their families entrust in me their mental and emotional health when I fully realized the privilege I was given. Opening up to me, revealing their innermost thoughts and feelings, including those often laden with shame and embarrassment, and allowing me to guide, advise, and join them in facing their fears is a privilege that I am grateful for every day. I cannot thank my clients enough for teaching me so much about the fascinating challenge of OCD and the strength of the human spirit.

I have a great team of my own supporters behind me. I am forever grateful to: Drs. Rudy Bauer, Bernard Vittone, Mary Alvord, John McPherrin, and Harvey Parker. A special thank you to Dr. Vittone for the medication chart included in this book. The love of my family makes me a better clinician in countless ways. Thank you to my husband, Brian, for supporting everything I do professionally and personally, and for calming me down when I've perhaps committed to too many things and perhaps have underestimated just how long those commitments would take. My two sweet boys, Isaac and Todd, create more light and provide more love than I ever dreamed was possible. I thank them for being so patient all those times I was writing. My sister of the heart, Emily's, endless enthusiasm for my work and belief in me as a person is an extraordinary gift. Thank you to Ilene, Norm, Lisa,

Aunt Karen, and Uncle Sandy for cheering me on and celebrating every achievement with such love, pride, and excitement.

My mother, whose love and presence in my life will never be gone, taught me everything I know about kindness, compassion, determination, and resilience. She loved me fully and completely, and inspired confidence in me to do whatever I set forth to do. She was both fascinated and proud of my work as a psychologist, and it is my hope that my work honors her memory.

Finally, I am so proud and grateful to work with Lacy Compton on yet another book! Her guidance and editorial excellence greatly contributed to this work.

Introduction

Welcome to *Parenting Kids With OCD*! If your child or teen has been diagnosed with obsessive-compulsive disorder (OCD), or you suspect your child has it, then this is the book for you. I wrote this book in a straightforward manner, with the goal that after reading it, you will have gained a comprehensive understanding of OCD, its symptoms, types, how it presents in children, and what effective treatment looks like. You will learn the specifics of how it is best treated, and how to best support your child as she works toward overcoming the disorder. Everything I explain is based on cognitive-behavioral therapy (CBT), which is the most empirically supported approach to understanding and treating OCD.

As a specialist in anxiety disorders and OCD, I know firsthand the intensity that is involved in parenting a child with OCD and how it can affect your every move. *With OCD, family accommodation is the rule, rather than the exception, and the more accommodations a family makes, the more stressed that family is and the worse the child's OCD gets.* Higher levels of accommodation are linked with a worsening of symptoms. For this reason, I have included clear recommendations for how to gradually stop accommodating and what you can do instead. By being sensitive and warm, yet firm and consistent, you will develop a better way of responding to your child's OCD, which will benefit everyone enormously.

You will learn about how to find the right treatment for your child, and strategies that you can use at home and at school. We will go through many case examples to illustrate the different types of OCD and to better understand the course of treatment. We will also discuss

DOI: 10.4324/9781003237044-1

when more intensive treatment options should be considered and what to expect in the future.

Because stress exacerbates OCD symptoms in children, we will devote some attention to stress management for your child and for you as well, as it tends to be a parallel experience. Finally, I've included a list of resources and helpful organizations, as well as additional readings in the Resources section at the end.

Chapter 1

Is It OCD?

Obsessive-compulsive disorder (OCD) has been identified and classified as a disorder since the very late 1800s. Beginning in the mid-1960s, behavioral approaches showed great promise for treatment, and by the 1980s, they evolved into cognitive-behavioral therapy (CBT), specifically exposure/response prevention (E/RP), which is currently used with great success in both the understanding and treatment of the disorder. By now, most cases of OCD are very treatable, and it is essential to have hope about your child's prognosis and his or her ability to succeed on the path toward improvement. This book is based on the principles of CBT, and my goal is for you to gain a thorough understanding that can then inform you when guiding your child toward improvement. Knowing the specifics of CBT will also help ensure that the treatment your child receives is both comprehensive and consistent with the approach.

Formally included in the category of anxiety disorders in the previous version of the Diagnostic and Statistical Manual of Mental Disorders (DSM; the bible for mental health practitioners that includes the criteria for all mental health disorders), OCD has become its own category called *Obsessive Compulsive & Related Disorders* (OCRD) in the current version, the DSM-V. This is due to the fact that OCD, unlike the other anxiety disorders, is linked with a host of other disorders, including body dysmorphic disorder (BDD), hoarding disorder, trichotillomania (hair pulling disorder), and excoriation (skin-picking) disorder, and that not all individuals with OCD actu-

 DOI: 10.4324/9781003237044-2

ally experience anxiety. Regardless of the new categorization, most kids with OCD are incredibly anxious about their OCD and, often, anxious in general.

OCD affects 1%–3% of children and adolescents; at least 1 in 200 children and teens in the U.S. have OCD (American Psychiatric Association [APA], 2013; Ruscio, Stein, Chiu, & Kessler, 2010). Although OCD can appear at any time during childhood or adulthood, it typically starts between the ages of 10–12 or during late adolescence/young adulthood (Greist & Baudhuin, n.d.). In order to meet the criteria for OCD, your child must have either *obsessions* or *compulsions* (although most children have both) that cause an interference or impairment in his or her life. Obsessions are persistent unwanted or intrusive thoughts, urges, or images that the person cannot ignore or suppress. For most people, the obsessions cause anxiety and, often, intense fear. Compulsions are repetitive behaviors, rituals, or mental actions that are usually performed in response to the obsessions:

> The behaviors or mental acts are aimed at preventing or reducing anxiety or distress, or preventing some dreaded event or situation; however, these behaviors or mental acts are not connected in a realistic way with what they are designed to neutralize or prevent, or are clearly excessive. (APA, 2013, p. 237)

The obsessions and compulsions must be time-consuming (take an hour or more a day) or they need to cause a significant impairment in the child's life (in academic, social, or other important areas of functioning). It is not necessary for an individual to have insight into the obsessions and compulsions (meaning that they don't have to be considered to be excessive or unreasonable to the child); however, most children find the obsessions and/or compulsions distressing and unpleasant.

Common types of obsessions include:
- ✧ contamination,
- ✧ repetitive doubting,
- ✧ desire for certainty,
- ✧ symmetry,

- ✧ "just feels right,"
- ✧ scrupulosity,
- ✧ unwanted sexual thoughts,
- ✧ losing control or doing harm, and
- ✧ indecisiveness.

Common types of compulsions include:
- ✧ washing/cleaning,
- ✧ checking,
- ✧ needing to ask/tell/confess,
- ✧ counting,
- ✧ ordering/arranging,
- ✧ repeating actions,
- ✧ waiting until or doing it over until it "feels right,"
- ✧ praying, and
- ✧ asking for reassurance.

In addition to the common types of obsessions and compulsions, there are types of OCD beliefs that define the person's experience with OCD. These include:

- ✧ **Overimportance of thoughts:** Thoughts can be experienced as powerful as action or truth. Often, the child will question himself, doubting who he is and believing the faulty and unwanted OCD thoughts reflect his true intentions. He will believe that having a thought about something bad happening means it will happen (these are called *fusion* thoughts, which are discussed further in Chapter 4).
- ✧ **Desire for certainty:** Wanting to know for absolute sure that something did or did not happen. Being totally certain is associated with safety, and anything short of that is typically considered risky. This thinking pattern is often at the root of checking and rechecking and repetitive questioning behavior. The persistent doubting results from not feeling certain that something was completed.
- ✧ **Overestimation of danger:** There is a magnification of the world as being dangerous and an exaggerated sense that some-

thing bad will happen or go wrong. There is an unrealistic belief that factually nondangerous behaviors could result in catastrophic outcomes; for example, the child may believe that she can contract a disease like cancer or HIV from actions such as touching a surface or being around someone who is bleeding. The child feels that there are things that need to be done in order to prevent harm, and the rituals can typically reflect extreme avoidance.

✧ **Overresponsibility:** The child believes that it is his responsibility to ensure that something bad doesn't happen or that others don't get hurt. Often, the rituals will involve excessive checking and taking preventative measures. For example, the child may take it upon himself to check the house for fire risks every time before leaving. Making mistakes can be perceived as a threat to one's safety, as the person feels (on a sort of karmic-level) that he will be to blame for hurting someone or getting someone sick, or if he did not take "ideal" measures to prevent illness or harm.

✧ **Perfectionism:** Not only does the child think it is possible to be perfect, but she also thinks something needs to be perfect in order to count. Often the child will do something and redo it many times in efforts to make it perfect. There can be an excessive concern about needing to know information, a fear of losing or forgetting something important, and an inability to delegate tasks or trust others.

✧ **Rigid/Moral thinking:** This inflexible style of thinking assumes that there exists a fundamental "right" and "wrong" in life. If something is done that could be considered wrong, the person feels he will be at risk for punishment.

✧ **Religious scrupulosity:** Feeling like they have sinned when no sinning has occurred. It is similar to overresponsibility, as the person feels a sense of responsibility if he or she puts someone "at risk" by not taking preventative measures, yet the responsibility is rooted in his or her worth and/or approval from God: "The French label the emotional condition which is part of scrupulosity 'the doubting disease.' This describes well the dilemma of the scrupulous. They feel uncertain about religious experiences and do not find reassurance through the normal means available to them" (Ciarrocchi, 1995, p. 5). A person can have scrupulosity without having OCD, but we will focus on it when it occurs as the main theme or type in OCD. In *The Doubting Disease* (Ciarrocchi, 1995), the author explained that there are several possible themes of scrupulosity: honesty, blasphemy (against God), cooperation in sin, sexual ideas (e.g., worrying about being lesbian or gay or being a cheater), and charity (e.g., where the person questions her goodness when it comes to serving others).

✧ **Sexual Obsessions:** This can be an extension of religious scrupulosity, or the sexual obsessions can occur outside of any scrupulosity. They can include preoccupation with sexual thoughts, sexual orientation, mislabeling normal sexual thoughts as perversion, thoughts about molesting other children or being a pedophile, or having sexual contact with someone inappropriate, such as a teacher or friend's parent. Usually occurring in older children or teens, these thoughts create a great deal of distress, including guilt, shame, and embarrassment.

Although the causes of OCD are not known, it does tend to run in families, implying a genetic component, although genes are not fully responsible for causing it (Greist & Baudhuin, n.d.). Sometimes, it can be associated with strep infections. PANDAS (Pediatric Autoimmune Neuropsychiatric Disorders Associated with Streptococcal infections) is caused by the body's response to strep infection, not the actual infection; therefore, it seems to be a faulty reaction of the immune system. A child can be diagnosed with PANDAS when OCD symptoms suddenly appear (acute onset) in a dramatic way, almost like the child developed OCD overnight. Often this diagnosis follows multiple strep infections. However, PANDAS has been expanded to Pediatric Acute-onset Neuropsychiatric Syndrome (PANS) as studies showed that PANDAS symptoms did not always begin after strep infection. Typically, OCD has a more gradual presentation; for example, a child may begin to express some extra concern about germs, ask a lot of contamination-themed questions, then start to wash a little extra, then show some avoidance of doorknobs and public restrooms or of eating food without washing her hands first, and then over months or years, it becomes more severe and time-consuming.

Children who receive the PANDAS diagnosis still need to undergo traditional CBT treatment for the OCD; however, the reason it is relevant to consider a PANDAS/PANS diagnosis is that additional treatment and pharmacological interventions (such as longer term antibiotic treatment, or in more severe cases, plasmapheresis, steroids, or intravenous immunoglobulin, IVIG) may be helpful. PANDAS is still being investigated, and there is some disagreement among clinicians in terms of its validity. From my standpoint, I am primarily concerned with the resolution of symptoms; therefore, when a child comes to see me for OCD treatment, regardless of if a PANDAS diagnosis has been made, I follow the same course of CBT treatment and get the same positive outcomes as those who come without it. Usually children are referred to me after receiving a PANDAS/PANS diagnosis, but sometimes I suspect a case of OCD may be rooted in PANDAS/PANS, and when this occurs, I will follow along with my typical treatment, but if after 3–4 months there is not enough improvement, I will refer out to specific pediatric neurologists who are careful not to overdiagnose the condition.

Sometimes obsessions and/or compulsions, or what may appear to be either, are symptoms of another disorder, so it is necessary to make a "differential diagnosis," which means that a diagnosis must involve consideration of what else it could be. Therefore, other diagnoses need to be ruled out. Body dysmorphic disorder (BDD) occurs when there is a preoccupation with one or more aspects of one's appearance that he or she perceives to be flawed; while the person is consumed with thoughts about it for at least an hour a day, the obsessions and compulsions are limited to a focus on physical appearance. With hoarding disorder, the symptoms are centered on difficulty with getting rid of possessions; there can be a compulsion to accumulate and save items, yet the focus is concerning the items (and refusing to part with them). It is also possible that the obsessive ruminations (recurring worries) are better explained by generalized anxiety disorder (GAD), which is when there is hard-to-control anxiety and worry lasting for at least 6 months that, again, causes an impairment in the person's life. For GAD, the person must have symptoms such as feeling restlessness, being easily fatigued, irritability, difficulty concentrating, muscle tension, and so on. One can also have GAD with obsessive features without meeting the full criteria for OCD. Other anxiety disorders, such as social phobia and separation anxiety disorder, may also need to be considered, as the repetitive fears about being judged negatively or about something bad happening to a loved one can resemble obsessions. Similarly, someone with major depression may ruminate in a way that appears obsessive (e.g., guilty ruminations); however, the thoughts are more reflective of the person's mood (mood-congruent) and not necessarily experienced as distressing. Also with depression, there tend to not be any compulsions.

Perfectionism may or may not be OCD. In some cases, perfectionism is its own problem, having little to do with OCD. Other times, it is part of the OCD, specifically the "just feels right" type. There can be an obsessive preoccupation with symmetry or order, which manifests like perfectionism, but the behavior associated with this preoccupation is really a compulsion (ritual). Finally, eating disorders can often present as OCD (e.g., ritualized eating behavior, avoidance of certain foods) but are limited to concerns about food and weight. When the disturbance of the obsessions and/or compulsions is better explained by one of these other disorders, then a different diagnosis is made. (This book focuses only on OCD; refer to http://www.iocdf.org for resources on these other topics.)

Alternatively, a child can meet the criteria for OCD and another disorder at the same time; this is called *comorbidity*, as both disorders are co-occurring in the child. For example, it is not uncommon for a child who has OCD to also have generalized anxiety disorder or social anxiety disorder. About 30% of children with OCD will also have an anxiety disorder, and often this is separation anxiety disorder (Boileau, 2011). Thirty-nine percent of children and 62% of adolescents will have symptoms of major depression at some point in the course of their OCD (Boileau, 2011). Tourette's disorder occurs in 25% of children and 9% of adolescents with OCD (Boileau, 2011). The studies range when it comes to ADHD, showing between 0%–50% comorbidity rates (Boileau, 2011). Although it can be discouraging for your child to be diagnosed with OCD and another condition, the good news is that CBT is also the most effective approach for all anxiety disorders and depression, with very good rates of success. It is just important that the treatment be targeted at the OCD and the additional diagnosis.

There are times when a child presents with OCD symptoms associated with an actual fear, such as food allergies. For example, children with severe food allergies are taught to take precautions and avoid contamination; it is necessary and crucial for them to learn how to prevent exposure to their allergens. Sometimes, though, the child develops excessive and interfering behaviors that go beyond reasonable measures (as defined by an allergist) to prevent potential contamination. An adaptive reaction may become an overreaction involving extreme avoidance and ritualized behavior, and sometimes OCD can develop. Children may be afraid to touch doorknobs because of a fear of coming into contact with nuts, when in reality, there is significantly little chance that a random doorknob will have traces of nuts on it, or that those traces would even induce a reaction. Regardless of the cause of the OCD symptoms, it is treated in the same way (along with regular consultation from an allergist), and the child learns to face his fears while adhering to reasonable guidelines to ensure his safety. It's about learning a balance (same with handwashing), as we will discuss.

Finally, OCD symptoms exist on a continuum, from mild and slightly interfering to severe and debilitating. There are also periods when it gets better and periods when it gets worse; it can ebb and flow. As we will discuss, when children are stressed, the symptoms may worsen and cause more of a problem. The priority is to have an approach for how to deal with the symptoms, so your child can learn how to not be affected or organized by the OCD. The goal is for one's well-being to not be conditional; this is why treatment is so important.

Chapter 2

Understanding Your Child's Experience

When a child has OCD, even in its mildest forms, it shapes her world. OCD creates an obstacle to being in the moment, free from anxiety and free from preoccupying thoughts or urges. Simple things become overly complicated. For example, walking out of the house can be enormously triggering, requiring a great deal of checking and rechecking that nothing will cause a fire, that things are in their proper place, and so on. Eating from a bake sale with friends can be a great challenge when your child is worrying that the baked goods are unclean and contaminated from potentially unsafe cooking practices. Doing homework can be nearly impossible for the child who feels he has to create visual lines between words (a less common symptom of OCD). Answering questions can be a challenge when doubts come up, and the child feels that she cannot know for sure if she did something or not. The dance between obsessive thoughts and urges and time-consuming rituals can seem to go on and on, requiring your child's full attention and dedication.

Many children feel that their parents and siblings, especially ones without OCD or anxiety themselves, don't "get it." Parents are often roped into the symptoms, requiring negotiations, accommodations, and compromises. This can create quite a bit of tension in the home. This tension creates more stress for the child, and then the OCD gets worse. It can also be an isolating experience; he may be the only one

       DOI: 10.4324/9781003237044-3

who feels this way, the only one who perceives a threat. Sometimes the child may get frustrated with others for not sharing the same concerns or seeing the threats he sees.

When you are the parent of a child with OCD, it can often be very difficult to relate or connect with his or her experience. The obsessive thoughts or compulsions can seem so irrational and illogical that it is hard to empathize or understand the degree of distress. In addition, the time it takes to complete rituals or work through the trigger can interfere with daily life, which can be frustrating; for example, it can result in being late, or your child might be unable to participate in activities with friends and family. Parents are often conflicted about how they should best respond: make the accommodations or challenge the unrealistic thinking. Typically, they vacillate between feeling two different negative states, one that comes from giving in and working within the control of the OCD and one that comes from responding with frustration and anger, and the resulting sadness that their child feels so misunderstood.

Psychologically, your child with OCD is struggling to feel okay, and that is probably the most important thing to remember. She is not trying to manipulate or control you based on her character or personality; behaviors that come across this way are either manifestations of the OCD or performed in service of the OCD. With OCD, there are conditions to feeling okay: The compulsions or rituals need to be done in order to alleviate the stress and anxiety that come from the obsessive thoughts, urges, or beliefs. Burdened by repetitive thoughts that she cannot stop from replaying over and over, it can be very hard to focus on schoolwork and socializing. In addition, she may judge herself, feel ashamed, or blame her parents for making her OCD worse.

There can also be what appears as an "addictive" quality to OCD (which is similar to an eating disorder) where the behaviors around the OCD feel like an addiction. The child may lie about or make up false excuses for her behavior, to protect her ability to do the rituals, and she may go to great lengths to perform the rituals (similar to people with eating disorders). This can be a particular struggle for families as they cannot understand, and often have not seen in their child before, the lying or deceitful behavior. It is essential to see this as a component of the OCD and not a reflection of your child's true nature.

The more that you learn about OCD from your child (and from this book) and communicate your awareness, the more connected he will feel to you. When you tell your child that you read all about OCD and approach him in a loving, nonjudging, and understanding way, you will help him to see that you are on his team. We will discuss how to best respond in a manner that both challenges the OCD and maintains a positive connection with your child in Chapter 6. But first let's learn the OCD cycle.

Hyman and Pedrick (2010), in *The OCD Workbook*, explained the cycle of OCD as:

1. Activating Event
2. Unrealistic Appraisal of the Event
3. Excessive Anxiety
4. Neutralizing Ritual

There is a pattern to OCD in how it gets set off (triggered), and the triggers tend to be repetitive in nature. First, something happens to trigger the child (activating event), then there is a thought about or urge associated with the event (unrealistic appraisal of the event), then the child feels distress and discomfort (excessive anxiety), and to alleviate the anxiety, a compulsion or repetitive behavior is performed (neutralizing ritual).

For children and teens, I have simplified the cycle to (see Figure 1):

1. Event
2. Thought/Urge
3. Feeling
4. Action/Ritual

To better understand the OCD cycle, let's go through some examples that illustrate the pattern of how an individual gets caught in the cycle.

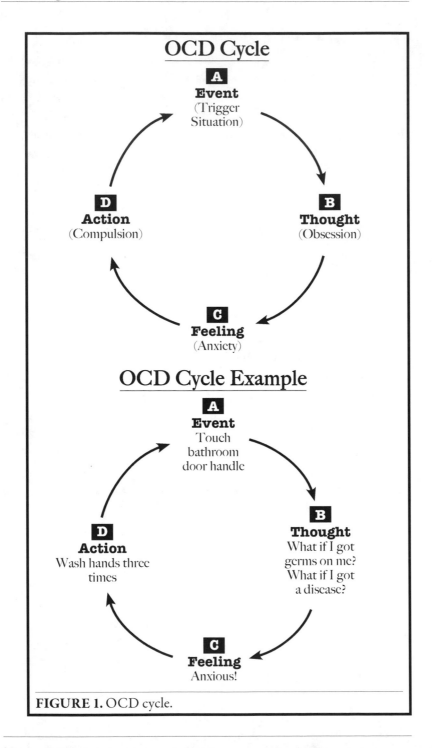

FIGURE 1. OCD cycle.

OCD Cycle Examples

1. Event: Someone nearby sneezes.
2. Thought: They are sick and now I'm going to get it.
3. Feeling: Feel anxious!
4. Action/Ritual: Wash hands and face, change into new outfit.

1. Event: Hear the word "cancer."
2. Thought: That's a bad word. What if someone I love got cancer?
3. Feeling: Anxiety and panic!
4. Action/Ritual: Repeatedly blink four times and tap thumb and pointer finger together four times.

1. Event: Step on something when walking.
2. Thought: What if it was a bug? What if I killed a bug? Maybe I meant to kill it. I'm a murderer!
3. Feeling: Anxious and fearful, physically shaken from remorse.
4. Action/Ritual: Go back and check for killed bug. Pray to God for forgiveness.

1. Event: Sit down at desk to do homework.
2. Thought: This all feels out of place—it's not right or straight, everything is imbalanced.
3. Feeling: Uncomfortable, "off" like left and right sides of body are not the same.
4. Action/Ritual: Move things around over and over until they feel "right" and appear straight.

1. Event: Start eating a cupcake from a bake sale.
2. Thought: How do I know if they used sanitary methods when making this? What if there are germs in here, or bugs?
3. Feeling: Anxious, disgusted.
4. Action/Ritual: Throw out most of cupcake and ask people at bake sale if they wore gloves when baking.

1. Event: Working on a group project with three other students; notice that one of the girls is very attractive.
2. Thought: What's wrong with me that I'm thinking bad sexual thoughts about her when we are supposed to be doing our work?
3. Feeling: Anxious, shamed.
4. Action/Ritual: Cancel social plans that weekend and stay in to study and "make up" for the project work that was missed from the "impure thoughts."

1. Event: Walking by a playground with children playing
2. Thought: What if I am a pedophile? Why am I looking at them playing?
3. Feeling: Anxious, guilty.
4. Action/Ritual: Turn the other way and cross the street. Avoid walking by in the future.

The OCD cycle reflects the cognitive-behavioral therapy (CBT) understanding of OCD. CBT considers OCD and anxiety disorders to have three components: physiological (body), cognitive (thoughts), and behavior (see Figure 2). The anxiety that comes from the OCD can often show up as physical symptoms: muscle tension, stomachaches, headaches, sweaty palms, restlessness, rapid heartbeat, and sweating. The thoughts include obsessions, worries, thinking errors (such as superstitious thinking), and negative self-talk. The behaviors include compulsions (rituals), avoidance, and nervous behaviors such as reassurance-seeking and excessive questioning. When we discuss how OCD is best treated, we will review these three parts again. For now, let's go through the three parts to better understand your child's experience.

Body/physiological. The opposite of being relaxed is being anxious. Sometimes anxiety symptoms are fleeting, with a start and an end to the physical change, such as a rapid heartbeat—the heart beats quickly, and then it stops and resumes a normal pattern. Other times, there is a chronic, ongoing sense of restlessness or being on edge—a

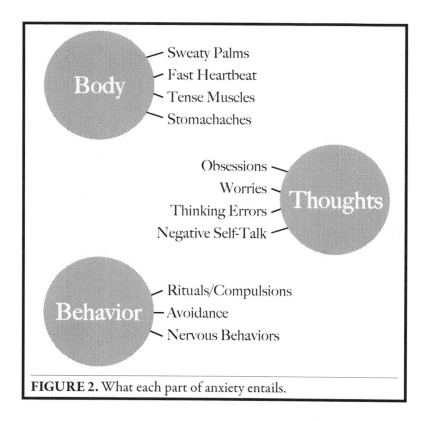

FIGURE 2. What each part of anxiety entails.

true inability to just *be* in a neutral physical state. This activation can make your child seem tense or jumpy, or just "on" at all times.

Thoughts. Obsessive thoughts are unwanted and intrusive, and they tend to go on and on and on, without the ability to stop them. The repetitive nature of the obsessions causes distress and occupies one's attention, making it hard to focus on much else. Worries and a preoccupation with doubt or uncertainty can make it hard to be present in the moment. Thinking mistakes (such as all-or-nothing thinking, magical thinking, and thought-event fusion) get in the way of seeing a situation in a reasonable, rational way and often trigger the OCD. Finally, negative self-talk can lead to self-doubt; for example, your child may repeat to himself, "I can't handle this," "I'm not okay," and "I have to go home so I can feel safe."

Behavior. Traditionally, anxious behavior is about avoidance. If someone is afraid of dogs, they will avoid being near them and may ask a lot of questions about possible contact with a dog (e.g., asking friends if they have a dog before they agree to a playdate) in the theme of avoidance. With OCD, there are plenty of avoidance behaviors (e.g., avoid touching doorknobs or using utensils that have come in contact with a table, avoid shaking hands with others, avoid social events or dating, avoid environments lacking in organization), but the primary behavior is a compulsion or ritual, an observable action or a mental action that the child does to alleviate the anxiety stemming from the obsession. Compulsions such as checking are done with repetition until there is a reduction in anxiety. The compulsion can also be a mental act, which, although not an observable action, is an action performed nonetheless.

The three parts work together as part of your child's experience with OCD. A thought may trigger the bodily symptoms of anxiety, and then the compulsions are performed while the thoughts are repeated. Chapter 4 explains that effective treatment addresses all three parts.

The following are quotes from children with OCD that help to explain their experience (*names and ages have been changed):

> I worry about killing something like by stepping on it. It makes walking around outside very hard and recently, I started wearing soft flip-flops only when I go outside. This way, I can see what's on the bottom because there are no lines or dents. I look at the bottoms to make sure I didn't step on an animal or a bug. When I come home I tell my mom about the different times I stepped on something at school that might have been a bug or an animal and I feel better when she tells me it wasn't. Sometimes I don't know if I stepped on a bug or animal and I go back and check the area. Also, I don't go on the grass or dirt at recess because I'm pretty sure I'd end up stepping on something and killing it. I also worry about this cat that I've seen in our neighborhood, and I'm not sure if that cat has a home so I keep putting out a bowl of milk in the back just in case.
>
> —Ali, age 9

My OCD is about getting sick and throwing up. This time of the year is the worst because people are sick all around me. I don't like to go to places where there are lots of people like the mall or the movies because most likely someone in the crowd is sick. I don't even like to go to a house party because there are so many kids in one small place. I also get stomachaches all the time and worry that it's the beginning of the stomach bug and soon I will throw up. When this happens, I don't like sitting in the middle of anything, like the inside of a booth, because if I need to throw up it will take longer to get out. I stay away from other kids who have recently been sick or if someone in their family had the stomach flu. I also use Purell and wash my hands frequently to prevent getting sick.

—Desiree, age 16

It's hard when people ask me questions. Instead of answering directly, I usually say "I guess," or "I'm not sure," or "I don't know," and this really drives my parents crazy. Sometimes it's embarrassing also because it takes me a long time to make decisions and even when I finally do, I keep thinking it wasn't the right one. My parents get annoyed with me and sometimes they just make the decision for me. I go back and forth and keep thinking of the good and bad parts of each decision, and how that decision will change how things turn out. I wish I could be like my friends who just decide and then move on, like they don't have to spend much time thinking at all—they seem to just know what they want and I wish it was clear for me like it is for them. I don't know why I don't seem to be able to make decisions, almost like I don't know myself very well. And even when I do finally pick, it still doesn't feel that great because I keep thinking about the other choice I didn't make.

—Nico, age 13

My parents called me a perfectionist for a long time before we understood it as OCD. I have to have everything perfectly organized in my room and I don't like when things are uneven or not straight. It's the same at school where I keep my belongings perfectly organized. I feel better when it's like that. Sometimes we may go somewhere, and I will have to leave because things there are not straight or aligned. When I go to bed, I have my Dad and Papa fix the blanket so that it's even on each side of the bed. Then I can go to sleep easily. I also can tell when they are getting annoyed with me and I like them to say things in a certain way. At bedtime, I need to say "Goodnight Dad, I love you," then he has to say, "Goodnight Sean. I love you and sweet dreams my boy," and if Papa is home, I do the same with him. If he rushes through it, I make him do it again or else I can't go to sleep easily.

—Sean, age 11

My OCD is the scrupulosity type. Before I understood it, I used to spend a lot of time worrying about being a bad person and that I would be punished by God. Anytime I had an "impure" thought, it would be followed by many other thoughts about how bad I was, that something was wrong with me or that I must be perverted or weird. It's a lot better now and I'm still in therapy. It has made dating a big problem as I don't feel that it's worth it to try to date a girl because it could trigger my OCD thoughts about being a pervert, so that is what I'm working on now. There is basically a list I have in my head of things I shouldn't do or think about because of what it says about who I am. When those thoughts come up, I do something "good" that helps to balance it out; so I might volunteer to help out at home, do a chore without being asked, maybe clean something in my room, or do some studying. When I do these good things, I feel it's helping to compensate for my bad thoughts.

—Chris, age 14

I often think "what's wrong with me?" My friend at school told me that she thinks she is really a boy and now I wonder if I feel the same way. I also worry that I'm a lesbian, but then I feel bad because there is nothing wrong with being a lesbian, and I don't think I'm a lesbian but many people really are, so I feel terrible that I am probably not one but worry I might be and then I feel guilty. Also, when my little cousins come over and climb on my bed, I think "What if I am going to molest them?" Then I have my brother come in the room too because I know I wouldn't do anything if he was there. Or I will sit on my hands because this way I know I won't touch them. I'd rather not be around little kids at all because I am so anxious about these thoughts and why I'm having them, because I don't think normal people have these thoughts.

—Ana, age 12

I feel scared a lot and have really bad thoughts. The thoughts are so scary that I will do anything to make them go away. I wash my hands a lot and my hands are always red and dry. Sometime they crack and bleed. I wish I could stop the bad thoughts from coming up at all. If I can't wash then I will wash double the next time, and when I can't wash I just put my fingers together in a special way and sometimes that helps. I don't want to talk about the bad thoughts or tell anyone about them because they are so bad.

—Kaitlyn, age 8

For many children and teens, they feel embarrassed about their OCD and label themselves as "weird" or "mentally ill," and these labels can be incredibly painful for them. OCD can bring about a deep sense of shame and isolation (maybe they do not know anyone else who has OCD) and can interfere with how they view themselves, ultimately affecting their identity. (In the next chapter, we will discuss the impact of OCD, including how it intersects with their development.) A major goal in learning how to manage and overcome OCD is for children to feel a stronger sense of confidence and ultimately resilience in themselves and what they were able to accomplish in terms of facing their fears. There is an expression I love: *Courage comes after slaying the dragon.* We want your child to develop this courage.

Chapter 3

The Impact of OCD

The impact of OCD is experienced by the child herself, but also by the family. It can interfere with family dynamics, creating tension in the home and between family members. The OCD can create obstacles to attending school, focusing on schoolwork, completing assignments, and participating socially. Depending on the age at which OCD begins during childhood, it can have a different impact on development. Erik Erikson (1963), a famous developmental psychologist, formulated a theory of lifespan development, divided into eight stages. At each stage, there is a "crisis," or challenge, and how one navigates the crisis of one stage will affect the ones in the future. During adulthood, for example, the crisis is "generativity versus stagnation." If resolved well and you have a sense of "generativity" from accomplishing (generating) your goals, whether that is in a particular career, getting married, or becoming a parent, you will be better able to resolve the next stage ("old age: ego integrity versus despair") successfully. So, if you have generativity in adulthood, it will help you have a better chance of having a sense of integrity for how you lived your life. The following are the three stages primarily affected by OCD during childhood:

- ✧ School age (5–12 years): Industry vs. inferiority
  - ⊚ Industry refers to a sense of capability (think about an industry that produces something) and a belief that they can succeed in the world. Inferiority represents a sense of self-doubt and feeling of inadequacy, especially in com-

DOI: 10.4324/9781003237044-4

parison to others. The overarching goal of this phase is *competence.*

✧ Adolescence (13–19 years): Identity vs. role confusion
  ◉ Identity describes who you are, what you are about, and attempts to answer the question of "What can I be?" It builds on the previous stage of having a feeling of competence (based on industry). The opposite of being clear about who you are is role confusion; when a teenager doesn't have clarity about who he is and doubts his decisions, he may have trouble forming a consistent self. This may interfere with developing meaningful relationships. The overarching goal of this phase is *fidelity.*

✧ Young adulthood (20–35 years): Intimacy vs. isolation
  ◉ Intimacy refers mostly to emotional intimacy (but physical as well), or the ability to be close to and vulnerable with another person. Can the person make a commitment to another and engage in a close, mutual relationship? Isolation is the opposite, and may be due to rejection or complicated by a lack of identity from the previous stage (e.g., when you are romantically rejected and you don't have a strong sense of self, the rejection can define you and then you become afraid of being vulnerable in the future, thus the isolation). The overarching goal of this phase is *love.*

It is important to consider your child's developmental stage in order to promote and encourage successful growth during the different stages, despite the OCD. This knowledge also helps you assess how the OCD is impacting him, and further highlights the importance of getting treatment. You want your child or teen to know himself outside of the OCD. He is a person first, and has a condition called OCD, which is second to who he is. It might be important to make extra effort to support his stage; for example, for the school-age child, you should help him identify hobbies or interests that he can work to succeed at, which allows him to experience his abilities and worth. Given that OCD (and anxiety in general) breeds self-doubt, it must be treated to prevent a sense of inferiority and, ultimately, poor self-esteem. Self-esteem is the greatest predictor of satisfaction in life and in relationships. For the child with OCD, it is important that the treatment process include working on positive self-esteem.

In addition to a developmental impact, children with OCD can often feel embarrassed or ashamed of their symptoms, may feel that something is "wrong" with them, and so on. It is of utmost importance that you do not support these beliefs and rather help them to understand that it's not their fault that they have OCD. It is important for you to help them define OCD as something to be treated and overcome. Emphasize that many other children have OCD (they just might not talk about it) and that having OCD doesn't make them "less" of anything (less normal, less likeable, less capable). You can also explain that, in fact, when you work through the obstacle of OCD, you learn what you are capable of and that you can handle anything that comes your way. This is how one develops resilience.

Your child's social life can also be impacted; in addition to worries about what other children may think if they see her symptoms, she may miss social events or not fully participate when she has the opportunity. On the flipside, many children with whom I work have very supportive friendships; they have been open about their OCD and have found friends to be incredibly understanding, loving, and respectful. Most of the time, the child's fears about being rejected or teased for having OCD are completely unfounded. This is particularly the case in adolescents, when most teens can have very strong empathy for their friends with psychological difficulties.

OCD can interfere in your child's academic life. Stress worsens the OCD symptoms, and when there is stress about schoolwork, it can be a double-edged sword (the academic stress plus the increase in OCD symptoms can make it very hard for work to get done). We will discuss how to support your child in school in Chapter 6.

When it comes to how families are affected, the conversation is mostly one about accommodations. As stated earlier, when it comes to childhood OCD, accommodations are the rule, not the exception;

up to 90% of families report at least some accommodation (Benito & Freeman, 2011). Accommodations are associated with a worsening of OCD symptoms for the child, and they create more family stress, specifically more functional impairment as viewed by parents (Storch et al., 2007). In fact, the degree of accommodations made by family members is associated with symptom severity and also with how well the child or teen will do in treatment (both CBT and pharmacological interventions like SSRIs). Reducing the amount of family accommodation results in better treatment outcomes (Benito & Freeman, 2011; Lebowitz, Panza, Su, & Bloch, 2012). One study showed that patients with OCD who did not benefit from CBT treatment had the highest levels of family accommodation compared with other participants (Ferrao et al., 2006). Essentially, family accommodation is an obstacle to the child's prognosis in treatment (Amir, Freshman, & Foa, 2000).

Family accommodation refers to how the family members participate in the child's OCD, whether they are also engaging in or performing the rituals with or for the child, supporting avoidance behaviors including avoiding anxiety-provoking situations, being willing to change the daily routine, or providing reassurance (Benito & Freeman, 2011; Lebowitz et al., 2012). The most common forms of family accommodation include providing reassurance, a family member's participation in performing rituals, and supporting the child in avoiding. For example, family members may directly participate in rituals: They may agree to wash their hands multiple times, may be the first to drink milk to make sure it is not spoiled, or may repeat a goodnight "I love you" in several different inflections until it "feels right" to the child. Parents and siblings can be viewed by the child as more trusted sources of "checking" and can do the checking behavior and report back that it is all okay (this behavior reflects both participating directly in the rituals and providing reassurance). I worked with a child with OCD who had refused to allow his family members to kill any bugs found in the home (out of fear of punishment by God), so his parents and sibling would "rescue" silverfish and other bugs, even though this went against their preferred practice of flushing the bug down the toilet or using bug spray. Basically, when you find yourself doing something that you normally wouldn't do on your own (for yourself) and that is in the service of the OCD, specifically for alleviating anxiety for your child, then you are accommodating! Although parents and other family members make accommodations out of love, warmth, and compassion (and usually a bit of desperation), it makes the OCD stronger and results in a worsening of symptoms.

Marital conflict can also result, as you may have one parent who gives in to the rituals and makes the accommodations and another who refuses to do so and blames the other for giving in. This dynamic (where you have one parent who is more permissive and one who is more authoritarian) is common whether OCD is involved or not, yet it can be exacerbated by the presence of OCD or another anxiety disorder. We will discuss how all family members need to adopt the same approach to dealing with the OCD and how family accommodation can be eliminated (see Chapter 6).

One study showed that the contamination type of OCD (e.g., washing symptoms) or a family history of an anxiety disorder were two factors that were related to more frequent family accommodation (Albert et al., 2010). Accommodations end up validating the OCD; after all, why are you rewashing your hands if there wasn't any contamination risk, or why are you saving bugs if there wasn't any risk of punishment? What families do to relieve the child's distress is only relieving it temporarily, in the moment, while it strengthens the OCD in the long run. It simply doesn't work. In the next chapters, you will learn that the goal is the opposite: Short-term relief is traded in for long-term relief. When your child or teen learns how to handle the short-term anxiety, stress, and discomfort that come from not performing the compulsions, she will learn how to become free from OCD in the long run.

Finally, extended family members may have a hard time understanding your child's OCD and its symptoms, or if they are not aware of the diagnosis, they may personalize or become upset in response. For example, if the OCD interferes with arriving on time to a family event or results in multiple trips to the bathroom to wash hands, without an understanding (based on OCD) of the conditions, they may be upset about the late arrival. This can, in turn, cause more stress for your child. Similarly, other caregivers (extended family, babysitters) can be frustrated and show lack empathy for your child, which can make him unwilling to be without you. This is why it is essential for extended family and other caregivers to be educated not only about OCD, but also about how they can best respond in the moment.

Chapter 4

The Treatment of OCD

This is the most important chapter of the book because it provides you with details on treatment of your child's OCD. In this chapter, you will learn the specifics of how cognitive-behavioral therapy (CBT) is used for OCD. As stated, the research shows that CBT is the most effective approach for treating OCD (and anxiety); in particular, Exposure/ Response Prevention (E/RP) is used to address the behavioral manifestations of the disorder. My goal is for you to be so informed and so clear about what effective treatment looks like that it will guide you in ensuring that your child's treatment provider is actually using CBT and giving your child every strategy possible to overcome her OCD. If you find yourself in the position in which you know more about CBT than your provider, it's either time to find a new provider or ask that yours receive training to use the best methods in working with your child (you can always give your provider this chapter to read).

There is no easy fix or quick solution for OCD. The treatment involves work, commitment, and regular practice with E/RP. With determination, however, OCD can be treated completely, or at least, symptoms can be so effectively managed that they no longer interfere with your child's ability to live life without impairment. Not all children with OCD are the same. Some will require additional treatment, such as pharmacological interventions, or more intensive treatment,

 DOI: 10.4324/9781003237044-5

such as inpatient hospitalization; guidance for this is included in the next chapter.

Successful treatment of OCD involves addressing the three parts: body, thoughts, and behavior. Most of the work is going to be on the thoughts and behaviors. The treatment process introduces strategies for each part, in order. I start by teaching relaxation and breathing strategies and other ways to calm the body, then move into the techniques used to address the thoughts component, and then while the first two continue to be practiced, I begin to help the child face her fears by doing the behavioral exposures.

Figure 3 includes an overview of the treatment techniques used for each part—we will go through each in detail.

Body:
◇ Calm breathing
◇ One-nostril breathing
◇ Progressive-muscle relaxation
◇ Exercise
◇ Yoga
◇ Meditation

Thoughts:
◇ Loop recordings
◇ Uncertainty training recordings
◇ Positive self-talk
◇ "Stamping" it "OCD"
◇ Distraction
◇ Identify and challenge cognitive distortions
◇ Detached mindfulness
◇ Attention training technique

Behavior:
◇ Create a ladder of anxiety-provoking situations in order from easiest to hardest (face your fears)
◇ Exposure/response prevention (E/RP)

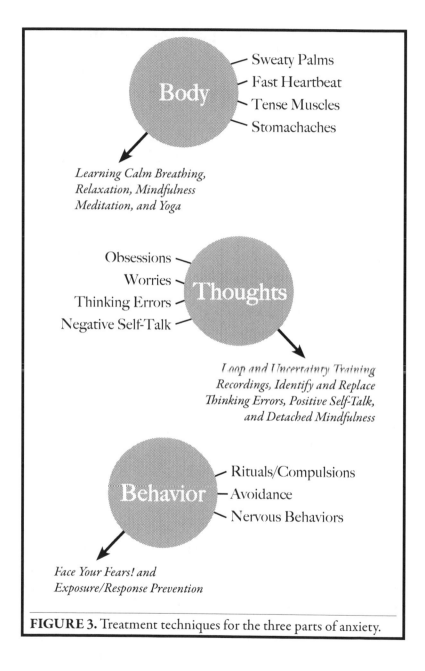

FIGURE 3. Treatment techniques for the three parts of anxiety.

Addressing the Body Symptoms

Calm Breathing

Many children with OCD have physiological manifestations of anxiety. They may seem on edge or restless or have a hard time winding down at night. Learning how to relax one's body and regulate one's breath is essential for managing stress and can also be useful when doing the E/RP work. To teach calm breathing, I have the child lie down on a yoga mat on the floor with a foam block placed on his upper chest. He should practice breathing in slowly through the nose and out through the mouth, allowing the air to travel all the way down to his lower belly, causing the lower belly to slowly rise and fall while the block on the chest remains still. Many children find that at first they have a hard time keeping the block still, or will push their lower belly out before the actual breath has entered into the belly. They should slowly inhale through the nose for the count of 4 and slowly exhale through the mouth for the count of 6 (it's better for the exhale to be longer than the inhale). With practice, they will learn how to keep the block from rising. This natural way of breathing (where the breath goes into the lower belly) is called *lower diaphragmatic breathing.*

One-Nostril Breathing

The second breathing technique is "one-nostril" breathing. I have the child hold one nostril closed while keeping his mouth closed, and then slowly breath in and out through only one nostril. Start with breathing in for the count of 5 and out for the count of 7, then gradually increase it to the count of 10 in and 12 or longer out. This pattern of breathing will force a calm breath, and doing this for 5 minutes leads to a physical state of deep calm. With both breathing techniques, it is essential to master them while calm (it won't work well if your child tries to do the breathing once he is activated or anxious). Once mastered when calm, he will be better able to know what he is aiming for (in terms of physical calmness) when he is anxious. These breathing strategies are particularly beneficial for children who have stomachaches and gastrointestinal issues as a symptom of their anxiety.

Progressive Muscle Relaxation (PMR)

Another technique to relax the body is progressive muscle relaxation (PMR). PMR is when you tighten and hold, then relax and release each muscle group in the body. The goal is to be able to notice when one's muscles are tense and be able to immediately relax them. Starting with her hands, have your child make fists (like she is *squeezing the juice out of a lemon*) and hold it for 5 seconds, then release it. Have her notice what it feels like when her muscles are tight versus when they are loose and relaxed. Using this formula of tightening-holding-releasing, while noticing the difference between tense and relaxed muscles, the child moves on to the arms, then shoulders, back, abdomen, legs, feet, and face; then, as a last step, the whole body all at once. With practice, children learn how to quickly relax their bodies and let go of any tension that they are holding onto. This gives them greater control over their bodies' responses to anxiety situations.

Exercise and Yoga

Exercise is another great way to release tension and manage anxiety in the body. Doing 20–30 minutes of daily cardiovascular training can be quite beneficial. It really helps with the mind-body connection, as working out the body usually clears the mind. Similarly, yoga is wonderful for kids with OCD. It teaches them to be still and in the moment, and to "unite" the mind and the body (the word *yoga* means "to join" or "unite"); a short routine of five poses in 15 minutes is a great starting point. For example, when a child is in a handstand against the wall, she is not thinking at all; rather, she is focusing only on doing the handstand and feeling what it is like to be fully in her body. Children 10 years old and younger may enjoy using *Yoga Pretzels*, which are colorful cards with easy-to-follow steps to get into a variety of yoga positions. Older kids may benefit from watching a video online or trying a teen yoga class.

Meditation

Finally, children who learn how to meditate will get to have the experience of suspending their thoughts while being in "being-ness" and hanging out in direct awareness. With practice, deeper states of awareness can be reached. There are many apps that can teach meditation (see the Resources section for a list). About half of the children I see embrace the recommendation to learn meditation; it's always worth introducing it, but do not be discouraged if they are not overly interested. At minimum, it suggests to them that they can experience a calmer state when they are not "in their mind" with their thoughts.

The main point of learning how to relax the body is to help expand the continuum between being stressed and relaxed. The more children practice how to relax, the easier it will be to return to a state of relaxation. It can also be helpful during E/RP when they have to tolerate the discomfort that comes from not engaging in the compulsion or ritual. It offers something they can do instead of the ritual.

Addressing the Thoughts Component

Addressing the OCD thoughts and learning a variety of strategies to challenge them is one of the most important aspects of treatment. The essential goal is to learn how to identify the OCD thoughts as "symptoms of OCD" and not real thoughts deserving of consideration. When the child can see the OCD as OCD, then he is able to fight it. Because OCD presents itself as regular thoughts, this first step of relabeling it as a symptom of OCD is key. Similarly, learning that thoughts are just thoughts and have no power unless we give them power supports this shift. Let's go through the various strategies designed to challenge the thoughts.

Loop Recordings

I used to call these "worry tapes" until cassette tapes became obsolete. Of everything out there to treat OCD thoughts, this is by far the most effective strategy. The child lists all of her OCD thoughts and worries, and then we type them up. The thoughts are written exactly how they sound in her head (so she would say, "What if I get sick from touching that?" and would *not* say, "Sometimes I worry that I'll get sick"), and then she makes a recording of the thoughts (usually using her phone or a parent's phone). Once she has a recording of at least 1–2 minutes, she begins to play it back in a row for 10–15 minutes every day. It sounds counterintuitive to do this, and most people worry that by listening to the thoughts over and over in this way, that the OCD will become stronger and the person will become more anxious. However, the total opposite happens: With repetition, the thoughts go from alarming to boring. After hearing herself say the thoughts over and over and over in this deliberate way, she eventually *habituates* to the thoughts. By hearing herself say the thoughts out loud, the OCD becomes "externalized," and this makes it easier to see the OCD as something other than herself. The child becomes an "observer" of her thoughts. And then, by listening repeatedly and hearing the thoughts over and over until they become boring and unalarming, she causes the thoughts to lose power. When making the loop recording, the child will often be scared or embarrassed to articulate her worries. Therefore, it is necessary to help normalize this exercise and validate the discomfort that goes into it. I usually say something about how if it's in her head, it is worth saying it aloud, or that it's in there anyway, and my office can be an extension of whatever it is that is on her mind.

Uncertainty Training Recordings

This is another version of the loop recording, except that you take the OCD thoughts and convert them to "uncertainty training" thoughts. For example, "What if I get sick from touching that?" becomes "It is always possible that I will get sick from touching that." The goal is to be able to tolerate not knowing for sure about something—to tolerate uncertainty (Leahy, 2006). OCD creates doubt and, at the same time, makes the person feel that he needs certainty. Checking and rechecking behaviors are performed in service of trying to know something *for sure*, yet the OCD is never satisfied and instead, the person gets stuck in the cycle of checking. When he learns to tolerate not knowing, and accept being uncertain about it, the cycle becomes irrelevant and the checking pattern is challenged. (And, of course, when this is paired with E/RP, the child practices the trigger on purpose—touching that surface or doorknob without checking it for germs or washing his hands—so the uncertainty training is done both cognitively by hearing the uncertainty training loop and then behaviorally by deliberately not doing the ritual of checking or washing and tolerating the uncertainty that comes from it.) After making a loop recording, I use the same typed list of thoughts and convert them into uncertainty training thoughts. Then I have the child make a recording of this as well, and the practice becomes listening to the loop recording followed by listening to the uncertainty training recording.

Let's go through an example, using both recordings, with a case already described:

I worry about killing something like by stepping on it. It makes walking around outside very hard and recently, I started wearing soft flip-flops only when I go outside. This way, I can see what's on the bottom because there are no lines or dents. I look at the bottoms to make sure I didn't step on an animal or a bug. When I come home I tell my mom about the different times I stepped on something at school that might have been a bug or an animal, and I feel better when she tells me it wasn't. Sometimes I don't know if I stepped on a bug or animal, and I go back and check the area. Also, I don't go on the grass or dirt at recess because I'm pretty sure I'd end up stepping on something and killing it. I also worry about this cat that I've seen in our neighborhood and I'm not sure if that cat has a home so I keep putting out a bowl of milk in the back just in case.

—Ali, age 9

Ali's Loop Recording:

What if I stepped on something and it was a bug or an animal? What if I injured it and now it can't walk? What if I killed it? What if I stepped on a bug and didn't know I killed it? I should go back and check to make sure. What if there are little animals on the grass that you can't see? You can't see the bugs in the grass. What if that cat dies because I never put milk out?

Ali's Uncertainty Training Recording:

It is always possible that I stepped on something and that it was a bug or an animal. It is always possible that I injured it and now it can't walk and it's all my fault. It is always possible that I killed it. It's possible that I stepped on a bug and wouldn't know that I killed it. It's always possible that if I go back and check I still won't see it and won't be able to know for sure. It's possible that there are little animals on the grass that you can't see. It's always possible that the cat will die because I never put milk out.

Ali listened to both recordings back-to-back; together they were a little under 2 minutes. She played the recordings for a total of six times each, which took about 11 minutes, and she did it every day. After 3 weeks, these thoughts no longer bothered her and they no longer occurred randomly, with the exception of a few times in which she was able to move past it quickly and shift her attention onto other things with ease.

The purpose of the loop recordings is to desensitize to the thought itself so the thought is no longer a trigger; the goal is *not* to desensitize or become okay with the *content* of the thought. The content of the thought is what they are worried about—the goal is not to accept or be okay with these bad things happening; rather, the goal is to become bored by the thought itself. The goal is to desensitize to the thought itself, regardless of the content. The thought, not the content, is the problem with OCD, as the thought keeps getting repeated over and over. It is important to understand this and also simplifies the treatment in a way, as it means that no matter what the content the thought is about (even if the content changes over time), one can become desensitized to the thought.

With loop and uncertainty training recordings, the child often makes several of them. At first, she'll have one recording, but then she will realize that other thoughts came up or that there is an area of the OCD she didn't do a recording on. Usually, she will create 2–3 additional recordings and then listen to all of them together. Once a recording is experienced as unalarming and boring, she can stop listening to that recording and focus on other ones. One important note about the "need to confess" type of OCD: It is important to limit the number of additional recordings the child makes to no more than 5 in total. We want to prevent the recordings from becoming a ritual, as the child may feel that the recordings are allowing her to "confess" or "tell" her thoughts or actions (and if she plays the recordings for you, that may allow her compulsion to happen, so she should have some recordings that you, her parent, never hear).

Positive Self-Talk

Positive self-talk allows your child to replace his OCD thoughts with ones that help to challenge the OCD and prevent compulsions. Unlike loop and uncertainty recordings, which are used at planned times other than during E/RP, self-talk is used *during* the exposures to help the child be able to cope with doing them. Also, your child should have some favorite self-talk statements that he relies on every day. The following self-talk statements help to reframe your child's experience with OCD (some are more sophisticated than others, and you can tailor the list to be appropriate for your child's age):

   ✧   I must face my fears to overcome them.
   ✧   I am uncomfortable, but I can handle it.
   ✧   I'm scared, but I'm safe.
   ✧   In the present moment, I am okay. Everything is fine.

✧ I can handle feeling anxious and I can handle what my body feels like when I'm anxious, or even sick. I can be okay in any situation.

✧ I can tolerate the discomfort that comes from facing my OCD.

✧ Anxiety is not an accurate (or good) predictor of what's to come. It's just an unpleasant feeling.

✧ It's just the OCD talking. Someone without OCD wouldn't be having this thought. It's just an OCD thought.

✧ It's just the OCD talking, so I don't need to listen to it.

✧ What would someone without OCD think in this situation? What would they do?

✧ It's me versus the OCD. Each time I listen to the OCD, it becomes stronger, and each time I don't, I become stronger. I must handle the temporary anxiety that comes when I do not give in.

✧ When I give into the anxiety, I am letting it run my life. When I don't, I regain control and become free to live my life.

✧ I cannot let OCD make decisions for me or control my life.

✧ I cannot allow OCD to influence my behavior or my family's behavior.

✧ What would someone who is proactive do in this situation?

✧ What is the proactive thing to do?

✧ I cannot react to the anxiety and let it control my life.

✧ I've never regretted facing my fears.

✧ I've never regretted challenging the OCD.

✧ Once I prevent the ritual, after a few minutes, the urge is gone and I'm fine. The hardest part is not giving in at first.

✧ Thoughts have no power unless I give them power. Thoughts are just thoughts.

✧ I can become an observer of my thoughts rather than a participant in them. I can see that it's "just a thought."

✧ I have to disconnect from the content of my OCD thoughts. I must see them and label them as a "symptom of OCD" rather than real thoughts deserving of consideration.

✧ I have to "sit with" and tolerate the discomfort that comes from not giving into the OCD.

✧ When I "sit with" and "tolerate" the discomfort, it goes away. Staying with the discomfort allows it to be metabolized.

✧ This is about tolerating negative emotions. I can handle whatever I feel. I don't need to be overwhelmed by what I feel.

✧ I have to tolerate the uncertainty of the situation and how I cannot know for sure. Some uncertainty is part of the normal life experience.

✧ Courage comes after slaying the dragon. Once I face my fears, I will realize I can do it.

✧ The goal is to not let any of these "thoughts" have any power in my life. This is about changing my relationship with my thoughts.

✧ Once I get good at labeling the thought as OCD and not focusing on the content of the thought, it won't bother me. I'm not afraid of the thought, and I don't give it any power.

✧ I have to expect that the thoughts will come up in my trigger situation. Expect it and plan how to respond to it without giving in.

✧ What can I do (what action can I take) in this moment to connect with something (an activity, a book, yoga, another person)?

All of this self-talk is designed to give your child or teen a sense of what to say in response to the OCD. This is how your child can challenge and "talk back" to the OCD, and self-talk can be used during the exposures. Knowing what the OCD sounds like and how it comes up and seeing it as separate from himself make him better able to challenge it.

"Stamping" It OCD

Once I have a sense of the different OCD thoughts the child has, I take a sheet of paper and write several of them down on different parts of the paper, leaving space between each. Then using a red Sharpie marker, I have them "stamp" the OCD thoughts by writing "OCD" over the thought, in big letters. When the thick red ink is written over the thought, it becomes hard to read what it says. Several clients have told me this is very helpful and that when they have a random OCD thought come up, they visualize "stamping" it with a big OCD stamp, enabling them to dismiss it. Once it's accurately labeled, children can become good at dismissing it. We are not trying to forget about the thought; we are trying to label it so we can dismiss it as irrelevant (and as only a symptom of OCD).

Distraction

In the moments when your child is either too activated to use any of the CBT strategies or when doing E/RP, distraction can be useful, as it helps him refocus temporarily on something else. Then he can return to the E/RP a bit calmer and better able to tolerate the discomfort. For example, a child may have thoughts about something bad happening to a loved one and perform the compulsion of shaking his head or tapping his fingers or doing some concrete behavior, such as washing his hands, in response to the obsessive thought. He learns that this behavior is OCD and that he has to challenge it by not doing the compulsions. Knowing this is the treatment plan may create heightened anxiety about having the bad thoughts. Therefore, before he can do the challenge, he may need to do a little distraction first. Generally, we want distraction to be used momentarily, with the goal of doing the real OCD work once he has calmed down a bit. Distraction occupies the mind and gives the body the chance to slow down and be calmer. Here are some distraction techniques:

- ✧ Use the ABCs to make lists: girls' names (Alicia, Bonnie, Camryn, Denise, Emily) or boys' names; fruit/veggies (Apple, Banana, Carrot, Date, Eggplant); cities/states/countries (Africa, Bethesda, Cuba, Delaware, Ethiopia); and so on. If the child is younger, she can just make a list for a category, without it being alphabetical.
- ✧ Lists of Five: five things that are green, five things in my backpack, five favorite books, five favorite musicians, etc.
- ✧ Playing a game or doing a puzzle such as a word search.

The distraction techniques should be easy to access and not require much in terms of effort or materials. Again, they are using it for just a short time period before doing the hard work of challenging the OCD. The reason for this is that we want your child to learn how to handle and tolerate the discomfort that comes from not engaging with OCD or its rituals. Avoiding the uncomfortable feelings is another form of avoidance and won't allow her to truly overcome the OCD. She has to be able to tolerate the unpleasant emotions, such as the anxiety, and habituate to those feelings in order to not get triggered emotionally anymore.

When looking at the techniques described thus far, it may be a bit confusing about how they are used and fit together, and also how to negotiate the natural contradictions of, for example, uncertainty training and self-talk. Essentially, all of these strategies should be learned, as they each have their place at certain times:

- Loop recordings and uncertainty training recordings are part of planned practices ("homework," if you will) that the child does to desensitize to his OCD thoughts and intolerance of uncertainty. When practicing the recordings, the child should find a time when he is not currently being triggered by the OCD, if possible. Usually done at home, he finds 10–15 minutes a day to sit down and listen to the loop over and over; after 2–4 weeks, he should desensitize to the recordings and find them boring instead of anxiety-provoking. You may need to sit with him at first to get him used to it and to help him deal with the anxiety that surfaces from hearing the OCD thoughts (again, for the "need to confess" type, make sure that they have at least one recording that you never hear). The overarching goal of the recordings is to be okay with the upsetting or anxiety-producing thoughts or uncertainty.

- Positive self-talk, on the other hand, is to be learned (and often memorized) during calm moments, but used during anxious ones, such as when doing E/RP. During the E/RP, the child says to herself something like, "I must face my fears. It's just the OCD talking, and I don't have to listen. It's just a thought, and thoughts have no power." Saying the self-talk allows her to be able to do the E/RP and face her fears without doing the compulsions. The self-talk, then, supports her and encourages her to manage the experience and make the necessary progress.

✧ "Stamping" the OCD should be introduced as an activity first. Then when the thoughts come up automatically, the child should either visualize stamping it or actually write it down and "stamp" it as "OCD." If OCD thoughts come up and your child is telling you about them, you can prompt the strategy by starting to write the thoughts down. Then give your child a red marker to have her write over the OCD thoughts with a big "OCD" in red ink. Again, this may be done at random times and either during or not during E/RP.

✧ Distraction, as explained above, is to be used temporarily to help him calm down or manage the anxiety that comes from doing the exposures. Once he feels stronger or calmer, then he can and should face the OCD head-on.

Identify and Challenge Cognitive Distortions (Thinking Errors)

In addition to the common themes of OCD (overimportance of thoughts, desire for certainty), most people with OCD make several thinking errors. Identifying thinking errors is another step in challenging the OCD and making the OCD thoughts lose credibility. Here are the most typical thinking errors of OCD:

✧ **All-or-nothing thinking.** Thinking in extremes, meaning that things are either perfect or a failure; there is no middle ground—it's either one extreme or another. This inflexible style of thinking is often seen in perfectionism, where things have to be exactly as the person wants them to be and thinks they should be (and she can keep repeating and fixing until they are "right"), or else she is frustrated, anxious, or will avoid the activity or whatever it is that she sees as imperfect. It can also come up with cleanliness and germs, where the person is extreme about cleaning or sees an entire building as contaminated, instead of just one part (e.g., the bathrooms).

⬧ **Catastrophizing.** Visualizing the worst-case scenario and thinking the worst is going to happen. This typically comes out as "What if . . ." thinking. The child may hear of a risk and overestimate the severity of it and the likelihood of it happening. For example, a child may hear that someone got hurt while skiing and then worry that she or a loved one will also get a head injury and become brain damaged when skiing. This thinking error creates a lot of avoidance and overreactive behavior.

⬧ **Selective attention.** Paying attention to certain information that confirms one's belief while ignoring evidence that contradicts the belief. The child may think that eating meat can cause you to die, citing examples of a few outbreaks of *E. coli* where a few people died; however, she won't consider how many people eat meat every day and are fine.

⬧ **Shoulds.** Making rules about how things *should* be. With OCD, these rules tend to be exaggerated and very strict; for example, "I should not pray for my family at the same time as when I'm praying for someone who is sick."

⬧ **Magical thinking.** Thinking some things, such as numbers, are lucky, while other things are unlucky. The person may do things in "fours," such as picking the fourth tissue or the fourth book in the row. She may see something as a bad sign or bad luck and then avoid it because of that belief.

⬧ **Superstitious thinking.** Thinking that by doing something, you will cause or prevent something from happening. For example, the person may tap each foot twice and feel that it will keep his family safe, or he may touch every surface in the room with the belief that it will lead to a good outcome or prevent a bad one.

⬧ **Thought-action fusion.** The child believes that if he has a thought or an urge to do something, then it will cause him to do it. For example, he will believe that thinking about hurting a sibling will cause him to do to it, and then he won't trust himself to be alone with his sibling. Or that just thinking about not turning off the oven means he will end up leaving it on, which will end up starting a fire.

✧ **Thought-event fusion.** The child believes that if he has a thought about something happening, then it will cause it to happen or means it already happened. One example of this may be a child having the image of stepping on an animal, then thinking this image means it happened and that he needs to go back and check.

In challenging the thinking errors, the child should learn which ones he uses most often and then come up with a new way of thinking in response. The goal is also for the child to eventually minimize the automatic thought by saying, for example, "Oh, there I go again, catastrophizing." With repeated practice of challenging the thinking errors and developing new behaviors in response to triggers, the brain learns new associations (and old associations get replaced, becoming obsolete). Basically, the thinking errors are like habits, and the child needs to learn new habits (new associations). As your child's parent, you can point out when you make thinking errors to normalize it and model being open to coming up with new, more flexible ways of seeing a situation (many of us do all-or-nothing thinking). The self-talk statement of "what would someone without OCD (or anxiety) think in this situation?" is a great way of minimizing the thinking error's validity.

Metacognitive Therapy

Metacognitive therapy (MCT), developed by Dr. Adrian Wells (2011), is a type of cognitive therapy that offers a great deal to those with OCD. There are two main techniques of MCT: one you want to know about and use with your child (detached mindfulness) and the other (attention training technique) that you should know exists as a potential resource if needed.

Detached mindfulness. This strategy is designed to change one's relationship with his thoughts. It teaches your child how to become aware (or mindful) of and separate (or detached) from his thoughts.

The goal is to learn how to become an *observer* of one's thoughts, rather than a *participant* in them. When you can see the thought as "just a thought" and nothing else, and also remind yourself that thoughts have no power unless you give them power, it allows for a different experience of the thoughts. It also makes it easier to not focus on the actual content of the thought and instead see the thought as a symptom of OCD. When your child "participates" in the thoughts, he gives the thoughts attention, credibility, and value, and engages in behaviors in response to them. When he switches into "observer" mode, he can see the thoughts as they are, without reacting to the actual content of the thought (therefore, no participation). This is how he will change his relationship with his thoughts (so the thoughts don't have any power). The purpose of detached mindfulness is to help your child reclassify, or recategorize, the OCD thoughts as "symptoms of OCD" rather than real thoughts deserving of consideration.

So, how can your child learn detached mindfulness? The method I use is to write 10 different thoughts on 10 different sheets of paper. Of the 10 thoughts, seven are neutral, nonanxiety-provoking/non-OCD thoughts (N), two are OCD thoughts (OCD), and one is an untrue thought (U). I mix them together, putting them in the following order: N, N, N, OCD, N, N, U, N, OCD, N. Here is an example of 10 thoughts in sequence:

1. My favorite season is summer. I love the feeling of being at camp. (N)
2. I can't wait to have winter break—we are going to Florida, and I'm so excited. (N)
3. I love the pizza at Pizza CS—it's so delicious! (N)
4. What if that cupcake has dirty germs and makes me sick and I throw up? (OCD)
5. I'm thinking of joining the environmental club at school. (N)
6. I hope to move up to my next belt in Tae Kwon Do this month. (N)
7. I'm wearing neon yellow socks. (U)
8. I love my brother—we have so much fun playing together. (N)
9. What if I got the flu from sitting next to that girl whose sister had the flu, and now it's on my clothes? (OCD)

10. Art is so much fun—the teacher really comes up with great projects. (N)

After the 10 thoughts are written and organized in the order out-lined, I have the child read the 10 thoughts three times in a row (quickly) and then say aloud: "I can see these are just thoughts. Whether they are true or not, anxiety-provoking or not, they are just thoughts. Thoughts have no power unless I give them power." The child then practices this 1–2 times a day every day for a few weeks, depending on the severity of the OCD (sometimes he will do it for longer). At any point, he can substitute the OCD thoughts for different ones to keep it current (if the thought he wrote down is no longer a trigger, for example). With practice, this will help your child become an observer of the thoughts and learn to not respond to them. He doesn't have to fear the thoughts anymore. Also, the content becomes less relevant, because he sees that all of the thoughts have the common element of being thoughts, so the specifics are not important. A 13-year-old with severe OCD with whom I worked practiced this technique and had the greatest feed-back, demonstrating his mastery. He said: "I think I got it. Now, when the terrible thoughts come up, I see them as if they are being typed out on a screen in front of me; I cannot really read them or know them, but I see it as just the OCD and it doesn't bother me anymore." This is the goal!

Attention training technique. This is the second of the MCT techniques that I use, and due to its time-intensive nature, I tend to use it as a last resort. However, I have found it to be extremely helpful, and it is also well-supported by research. Attention training technique (ATT) is a 12-minute audio recording that is listened to while staring at a dot on the wall; ideally, the child or teen listens to the 12-minute long practice twice a day. The audio recording script (which is printed in Dr. Wells's book *Metacognitive Therapy for Anxiety and Depression* and also found on the MCT Institute website; see references) instructs the child to focus on different sounds, then to switch his attention from one sound to another, and then to count all the sounds he hears at the same time (during which all of the previous sounds occur at the same time). With repeated listening, your child is trained to easily switch from one thought (sound) to another, which addresses the common problem of being stuck, or locked into, a thought. Dr. Wells (2011) considered OCD to be a "cognitive attentional syndrome" in which the person's attention gets stuck on an unwanted or anxiety-inducing thought. The techniques of MCT have the goal of getting the person unstuck and free from the cycle of rumination.

Understanding the OCD Cycle

In addition to all of these techniques to help with the thoughts component, it is important for the child to gain a thorough understanding of the OCD cycle. Understanding the cycle will help her to externalize the OCD and lead to greater awareness of the OCD. As you see her getting triggered and performing the rituals, it can help to point out and even write out the cycle so she can gain more insight into the pattern. For instance, you can discuss the trigger, her interpretation or thought, how she felt, and what she did in response.

Addressing the Behavior Component

The behavioral manifestations of OCD include compulsions, rituals, and avoidance behavior. Additionally, children with OCD often seek reassurance (usually from a parent or caregiver) and ask a lot of questions. If the child with OCD is unable to avoid a trigger, he will endure it with quite a bit of distress and may do a compensatory ritual later on. If unable to perform a compulsion, he may become agitated.

Compulsions and rituals can be obvious or subtle. Most parents are surprised to discover the extent of the compulsions and how much mental space they occupy for the child. When learning the OCD cycle, the child sees the connection between triggers, thoughts, anxiety, and rituals (compulsions). The compulsions are typically performed in response to an obsessive thought, image, or urge, and they offer immediate relief for your child. This immediate relief ends up ensuring long-term OCD (so it's short-term relief, long-term OCD). A primary goal in therapy is for your child to understand that when the compulsion is prevented, the immediate relief is replaced with short-term anxiety; however, with regular practice of preventing the compulsion, the child overcomes the OCD. So short-term relief is traded for long-term relief and success. It's traded for freedom. This is important because the child will need to have a rationalization to rely on for why she is going to purposely cause anxiety and discomfort for herself. Tolerating the discomfort is the key and is necessary for success; it's about facing your fears and staying with it, despite the unpleasant experience.

It is important for children and teens to understand the *face your fears* mindset and why it is a necessary part of the treatment process. The compulsions, rituals, and avoidance all strengthen the OCD. When your child learns to adopt the "face your fears" mindset, and understands that it is "me versus OCD," he can start to challenge these behaviors. Exposure/Response Prevention is the choice strategy to helping the child with OCD. This is the "facing your fears" part, and it involves purposely exposing the child to a trigger situation and then teaching him how to prevent doing the ritual or compulsive behavior. An important principle to keep in mind when doing E/RP is something I borrow from a type of therapy called Acceptance and Commitment Therapy (ACT)—the "acceptance" part, which means

> opening up and making room for painful feelings, sensations, urges, and emotions. We drop the struggle with them, give them some breathing space, and allow them to be as they are. Instead of fighting them, resisting them, running from them, of getting overwhelmed by them, we open up to them and let them be. (Harris, 2009, p. 9–10)

The child has to learn how to "sit with" and tolerate the discomfort that comes from not performing the rituals or typical response to the trigger. Learning how to deal with the uncomfortable feelings, and seeing that after a while, the anxiety goes down and the urge to perform the ritual goes away, is a necessary component. *Habituation* occurs when the child stays in the situation long enough to get used to it. This is why the practices should gradually build up to being longer in duration, so the habituation happens. The child also needs to be able to realize that she can actually prevent herself from doing the ritual and that she is capable of facing her fears. It is not until she learns how to face her fears and tolerate the resulting anxiety that she will have the confidence to do so again and again (remember, courage comes *after* slaying the dragon). This is a boost to her self-esteem and a real triumph over the self-doubt that results from the OCD and is how she will overcome it.

To start, I have the child list her trigger situations, and I convert them into specific practices. For example, a trigger might be using public bathrooms, so the specific practice would be "walk into a public bathroom and touch the faucet with your hands." Once we have created a list of as many trigger situations, she can come up with, she puts them in order from easiest to hardest. I will have her look at the list and say "Okay, which is the easiest one to do?" and she will put a "1" next to it, then "Which is the hardest one on this list? The one you couldn't imagine doing?" and for a list of 22 items, she will put a "22" next to that one. Then she goes from there, ordering each item with a number in between. Using the list, we create a "ladder": On a poster board, I draw a ladder with rungs and write each situation on a step, with the easiest one at the bottom and the hardest one at the top. As she starts facing her fears, I put stickers on the ladder (up to two for each step: one on the left side once she has practiced that step once, and a second sticker on the right side once she has mastered the step from repeated exposure and it has now become part of her normal repertoire of behavior). This tracks her progress and rewards her success. (By the way, I use stickers with my adult clients as well, so I consider it an "all ages" practice.)

The following is a sample of a ladder (again using Ali's case of OCD); the hardest items are on the top and easiest ones are on the bottom:

(top)	Wear boots and walk on the grass/dirt without going back to check if you stepped on a bug or animal.
	Wear flip-flops and walk on the grass/dirt without going back to check if you stepped on a bug or animal.
	Wear boots and walk on the grass/dirt after seeing a bug in the grass without checking the bottoms afterward.
	Wear boots and walk on the grass/dirt without checking the bottoms.
	Wear boots and walk on the grass/dirt (can check bottoms).
	Wear boots when walking outside without checking the bottoms.
	Wear boots when walking outside (can check bottoms).
	Wear flip-flops and walk on the grass/dirt without checking the bottoms afterward.
	Wear flip-flops and walk on the grass/dirt (can check bottoms).
	Don't put milk out for the cat.
	Put milk out for the cat once a week.
	Put milk out for the cat every 3–4 days.
	Put milk out for the cat every other day.
(bottom)	Come home and don't tell Mom about anything you stepped on or where you walked.

You will notice that we broke larger steps into smaller ones, all of which made the exposure work possible and manageable for Ali. I also reminded her that we would go at her own pace, and as long as we were moving forward by doing some practice, she would make progress. I tend to gently push my clients to work on the steps and do as many of them as possible. With Ali's case, we did all of the exposures together, except for not telling her mother and the ones involving the cat. And to help prepare her for not telling her mom, we made a recording of about 3 minutes of her talking about her day at school and what she was looking forward to at school, none of which involved talking about where she stepped or walked. Her mom played this recording once Ali got in the car for the drive home from school; this allowed Ali to disrupt the ritual and replace it with a different dialogue. She used self-talk cards to help with doing the cat practices. By doing the other steps with her, I was able to help her manage the discomfort and prompt her to think differently about the OCD. In addition, my presence increased her sense of accountability to do the steps, and I was able to remind her of the value of doing the E/RP in the moment.

There are three keys to facing one's fears: repetition, frequency, and prolonged time. The child repeats each step over and over until he masters it; the practices should occur frequently together (every day if possible); and the child needs to stay in the situation for a prolonged period of time for habituation to occur.

There are a few additional mindsets that can be helpful to offer children as they are doing the exposures. First, I like to talk about the concept from the well-known childhood story *We're Going on a Bear Hunt*, where the father and his children travel through obstacles, and for each one, there is no way out but through: "We can't go over it. We can't go under it. Oh no! We've got to go through it!" (Rosen & Oxenbury, 1997, pg. 2). This echoes the "acceptance" part of tolerating the discomfort and reinforces the idea that the only way to get out of OCD is to actually go *through* facing one's fears. Second, I like to explain the difference between being *proactive* and *reactive*; in the 2014 book *The 7 Habits of Highly Effective Teens* by Sean Covey (the son of Stephen Covey, who wrote *The 7 Habits of Highly Effective People*)—a book I often recommend to clients 12 and up—it is explained that reactive people make decisions based on how they feel, while proactive people make decisions based on their values. OCD, by nature, encourages children to be reactive: They make decisions and their behavior is based upon their feelings (anxiety, uneasiness, discomfort, sense of doom). When we help them identify with the value of overcoming

OCD and being liberated from its control, they can use that to guide their behavior. Facing one's fear is being proactive. You can offer up a simple analogy to explain proactive and reactive: When it comes to homework, your child may not *feel like* doing it, and if he skips it, then he will have been reactive because he let his feelings decide. However, if he recognizes that he doesn't feel like doing his homework, but really *values* coming to school the next day prepared and showing respect to his teachers, etc., then he will do the homework even though he doesn't feel like it. In other words, the feelings are still there, but they don't decide or influence the behavior; the child isn't organized by his feelings. The behavior and the decision of what to do is guided by the person's values. For the child with OCD, we want to him to value overcoming it and becoming free of its control over his life. Third and lastly, I like to think about giving in or not giving in to the rituals as accumulating savings in a bank account. Each time the child does a ritual, he uses some of the savings, and this also results in not adding more money to the account. Each time he prevents a ritual, he preserves the money. Each time he purposely faces his fears and does E/RP practice, he adds more money to the account. So, there is merit in not giving in and even more merit to practicing on purpose. For some kids, it's useful for them to see it this way, and this can help them be more committed to not doing the rituals. Also, sometimes they aren't ready to fully face their fears but were able to prevent a ritual, and we want them to feel good about this and see it as an accomplishment. They might feel that they weren't able to do an exposure, but they still did something hard by not doing the ritual (they preserved the money).

Another important factor in working with the behavioral component is helping the child find the right balance when it comes to something that may be a ritual but is also something she still has to do. For example, when it comes to handwashing, the child with OCD who has excessive handwashing (typically resulting in dry, cracked skin) still needs to wash her hands every day. She can't completely avoid washing her hands, yet she almost can't trust her own judgment about when it's appropriate to wash, because it is too heavily influenced by the OCD. In this case, we want to give the child clear rules and set times when she should wash her hands, and help her to only wash her hands at those times. So, it might be that she only washes her hands before meals and after she uses the bathroom. (At the same time that she is learning these guidelines, she is also doing E/RP focused on handwashing: She may have steps on eating with unwashed hands, using the bathroom and only quickly rinsing with water, or using a portable toilet and not washing hands at all afterward.) But the guidelines of when to wash her hands on a day-to-day basis should reflect what "someone without OCD would do," and it should never result in dry, cracked skin.

Another example is the child who has food allergies but also OCD; he has a similar dilemma in that he needs to engage in avoidance behaviors for his health and safety—he cannot touch nuts, for example—yet it may be extreme in that he won't touch a countertop that was touched by someone who had eaten a handful of nuts yet has no nut pieces on it. The fear of surfaces and doorknobs that he worries may have been touched with nuts will mostly likely never result in an allergic reaction (always check with an allergist first, of course, but from my multiple collaborations with allergists and from having a son with nut allergies, I have been informed that these rather benign behaviors typically never result in a contamination). The balance here, again, is that he has to avoid contamination with his allergen, but he doesn't have to avoid being around someone who has eaten nuts, or touched a surface after handling nuts, for example.

Finally, an essential part of addressing the behavioral part of OCD is working to eliminate accommodations made by family members. The goal is to integrate steps to reduce and eventually stop family accommodations into the ladder. For example, there could be steps to challenge a rigid bedtime routine of saying, "I love you" in a certain way, and the parent receives guidance on how to modify the routine. We will focus specifically on family accommodations in Chapter 6.

We've now gone through the treatment protocol for overcoming OCD. Again, this is all based on cognitive-behavioral therapy, which is solidly supported by research as the best and most effective approach for treating OCD. In addition to these techniques, there are also pharmacological options. I prefer that a child or teen receive a proper course of CBT before considering medication; however, many children are prescribed medication as a place to start. The most common medications used to treat OCD are SSRIs (such as Prozac and Zoloft). Benzodiazepines and antipsychotics may also be used. More information on medication options, including those used for PANDAS/PANS, is discussed in Chapter 5.

Getting Help

Finding the Right Therapist

The most important decision you will make in getting your child help is finding the right therapist. What makes a therapist the "right" one? When it comes to treating OCD, the first basic qualification is that the therapist is trained and skilled in cognitive-behavioral therapy, with experience in treating OCD. I believe the majority of therapists are well-intentioned and have a true desire to help; they've devoted their career to a helping profession, after all. However, the reality is that many therapists and psychologists say they "do CBT" or "integrate CBT" into their work, and what this translates to is a basic explanation of thinking errors or teaching relaxation. The majority of therapists have received a more traditional (psychodynamic) education, which focuses on *why* the child has the OCD and what the experience is like for him or her. With this approach alone, the child will feel quite understood and emotionally supported, yet she will not be equipped with tools for what to do about it; it is not the same as CBT, which tends to be more solutions-oriented, filled with strategies and techniques.

When it comes to effective OCD treatment, the therapist must have a mastery of CBT and be able to provide the child with many of the strategies explained in the previous chapter. From my experience, loop recordings and E/RP are the two essentials. The research is clear: E/RP is needed to overcome the OCD. Many therapists talk about what the child can do to face his fears and resist the urge to do the com-

 DOI: 10.4324/9781003237044-6

pulsions, but what is essential is to have a clear plan with clear goals and a therapist who can perform as many of the exposures with the child as possible. When it is written down (for me, I prefer it in a ladder form, which offers a visual and indisputable measure of progress), it increases the sense of accountability the child has to do the exposures.

Another essential characteristic is that the therapist be warm and encouraging. Given that most children and teens with OCD are embarrassed about their symptoms, a therapist who is warm and accepting will make it easier for them to reveal their thoughts and work through the exposures together. Ideally, he or she will have a non-shaming demeanor and will help normalize the child's experience with OCD. In addition, we want the therapist to be confident in the techniques and be able to gently push your child to do the exposures. Some patience is required, but once the tools are taught, the child can benefit from solid encouragement. Even if a step needs to be broken down into smaller steps, we want to expect the child to work toward facing her fears. I often ask, particularly if a child is resisting, "What are you willing to do? What is a small step we can practice?" This puts her in a position where she needs to decide on something that she is willing to do. A therapist who is skilled and confident in the approach can assure the child about the effectiveness of the treatment approach. On a daily basis, I remind my clients about the strength of the work we are doing: "This works. It's as simple as 'if A, then B': If you face your fears, you will overcome your anxiety. It's you versus the OCD—don't give into it." They usually are doubtful (OCD breeds doubt and uncertainty), plus they have the OCD voice in their heads and it is very strong, but our voice (the therapist's, the parent's, and ultimately, the child's) needs to be stronger and louder!

So far, we have the first two qualifications: (1) strong CBT skills and (2) warm, accepting, and confident in the approach. A third qualification is the therapist's willingness and ability to guide you as parents in how to respond to the OCD. Given how family accommodations are the rule, rather than the exception, receiving guidance on how to pull back, how to support the exposures, and so on, can really benefit the process. This book is your guide and you can rely on it; however, it would be ideal for the therapist to give specific recommendations as well.

Once you get a referral, which you can get from your child's pediatrician or other parents of children with OCD and anxiety or by referring to the Resources list in the back of this book, you should screen the potential therapists to identify the best match. The International OCD Foundation (IOCDF; http://www.iocdf.org) has an excellent list of questions (under "OCD in Kids") to ask potential therapists, amongst other helpful guidance. When screening (talking to and possibly meeting with) potential therapists, it is essential that you ask them if they are "skilled in CBT" and ask them to describe their approach in treating OCD. It is also useful for you to ask them how they measure progress to "know if the therapy is working" or if your child is "getting better." You can gauge on the phone if they sound warm, but it's really up to your child to confirm this for you, once he has met with the therapist.

A question that I often get from parents when I give talks on anxiety is: "How do I know if the therapy is working?" One obvious sign is if your child is doing less of the compulsions and rituals, and if there is less interference in the daily routine. A child who was taking an extra hour to leave the house (due to checking behavior or doing her hair over and over) who can now leave after 30 minutes is making progress. A child who had to count each step she took or walk in a certain way who is now walking while talking or able to walk in a typical fashion is making progress. Another way of measuring is to use the ladder approach and note the progression with stickers (or checks next to each step); this not only shows what exposures she has practiced or mastered, but it also allows the child to see what she has accomplished, which is good for the momentum of doing the hard work of E/RP. It also helps her to see that if she was able to do one step that she previously identified as a trigger, she should be able to do the next one. Basically, the ladder helps build her confidence in the process of overcoming her OCD.

Treating OCD With Medication

The typical first step is to get your child into therapy with a CBT therapist. But sometimes your child will need more support, such as medication. The decision to medicate is often hard for parents, but medication can be very effective. Typically, I suggest starting therapy first, and if the child is not making any progress after 3 months or so, or she is having a hard time doing the exposures and the progress is quite slow-moving, then it is reasonable to consider medication. Also, if there is a strong family history of OCD or anxiety or depression, that is another indication that the child may benefit from medication.

Medication should be prescribed by a child psychiatrist. The most commonly prescribed medication is an SSRI (selective serotonin reuptake inhibitor), such as brand names Prozac or Zoloft, or the TCA (tricyclic antidepressant) brand name Anafranil. SSRIs are considered antidepressants, but they are very effective at treating anxiety and OCD. An SSRI prevents (inhibits) the reabsorption (reuptake) of serotonin and norepinephrine from the transmitting neuron (by binding to the transmitting neuron's receptors), which results in more serotonin floating around in the brain. For some unknown reason, when there is more serotonin floating around, anxiety symptoms improve. Anafranil is well-established as an effective medication for OCD specifically, but because it acts on more than just serotonin and norepinephrine, it tends to cause more side effects. Other times, your child may be prescribed a benzodiazepine, such as brand names Klonopin or Xanax, but usually this is on a short-term basis due to the potential for withdrawal symptoms; for example, if your child is unable to sleep at night because of OCD or anxiety, a benzodiazepine will help her to relax and go to sleep (benzodiazepines act on GABA, which is a neurotransmitter that causes the relaxation response, and the side effect is drowsiness, which is a good side effect to have at bedtime). Unlike SSRIs, which take 2–4 weeks to start working, benzodiazepines work immediately (and for this reason they can sometimes be used for a few weeks until the SSRI takes effect). Finally, some children may require an additional very small dose of an atypical antipsychotic medication, such as brand names Abilify or Risperdal, which can often help an SSRI work better; I only see these medications being prescribed in more severe cases of OCD and usually for a short-term (3–6 months) period to help the child or teen get through a more severe phase of the OCD. It may sound scary to take an "antipsychotic" medication; however, the dose prescribed for OCD is so small that it would not benefit someone with psychosis, yet it is often extremely beneficial for OCD symptoms. These medications work on a different neurotransmitter than SSRIs; they work on dopamine in the brain.

Table 1 provides a chart of the common medications prescribed and the side effects of each class.

If your child is prescribed medication, he should be in therapy at the same time. CBT or CBT plus medication has been shown to be effective (Walkup et al., 2008). Research shows that individuals with OCD who only take medication (without conjoint therapy) will show less improvement than when therapy is co-occurring. Some studies have shown that CBT alone leads to better long-term improvement and lower rate of relapse (Barlow, 2004; Hollon, Stewart, & Strunk, 2006). Also, children who believe it was the medication (and not a combination of medication plus their efforts) that improved the OCD tend to form a different understanding of what it means to have OCD. For instance, they may believe it is more of a "chemical imbalance" that they have little control over. Rather, we want them to learn strategies to overcome the OCD and see that those efforts lead to results. We want their efforts to be a part of them becoming resilient and stronger from overcoming obstacles (in this case, the obstacle of OCD). Also, we want the medication to be time-limited, if possible. Once the OCD is effectively treated with CBT and they no longer have symptoms of OCD, they should be slowly weaned off. Most of the children I work with who take medication are successfully weaned off without having symptoms return. For instance, when the symptoms come back, I will often increase the therapy back to weekly (as I slow them down to every 2–4 weeks once symptoms improve) and do more E/RP work; if after a few months, the symptoms persist or are getting worse, the child will go back on the medication for a longer period before trying to go off it again.

For PANDAS/PANS cases, a pediatric neurologist is typically needed. As explained, children diagnosed with PANDAS/PANS

TABLE 1
Antianxiety Medications

Type	Brand (Generic) Name	Side Effects
Antidepressants		
SSRIs	Brintellix (vortioxetine) Celexa (citalopram) Lexapro (escitalopram) Luvox (fluvoxamine) Paxil (paroxetine) Prozac (fluoxetine) Viibryd (vilazodone) Zoloft (sertraline)	Common: low sex drive, delayed orgasm Occasional: stomachaches, diarrhea, tremor, initial increased anxiety, agitation, irritability, headaches, sedation, trouble sleeping
SNRIs	Cymbalta (duloxetine) Effexor (venlafaxine) Pristiq (desvenlafaxine)	Same as SSRIs
TCAs	Anafranil (clomipramine) Elavil (amitriptyline) Pamelor (nortriptyline) Tofranil (imipramine)	Dry mouth, constipation, dizziness, tremor, sedation, anxiety, weight gain, hypotension
Other	Desyrel (trazodone) Remeron (mirtazapine) Serzone (nefazodone) Wellbutrin (bupropion)	Desyrel (trazodone): drowsiness, priapism (erection that will not go away) Remeron (mirtazapine): drowsiness, weight gain Serzone (nefazodone): drowsiness, irritability Wellbutrin (bupropion): irritability, insomnia, anxiety, dry mouth, weight loss, constipation
Antianxiety		
Benzodiazepines	Ativan (lorazepam) Klonopin (clonazepam) Valium (diazepam) Xanax (alprazolam)	Drowsiness, fatigue, lethargy, impaired coordination, memory problems, withdrawal symptoms

TABLE 1, *continued*

Type	Brand (Generic) Name	Side Effects
Beta Blockers	Inderal (propranolol) Tenormin (atenolol)	Lightheadedness, exercise intolerance
Other	Buspar (buspirone)	Dizziness
Atypical Antipsychotics/ Mood Stabilizers (often used to enhance effectiveness of antidepressants)	Abilify (aripiprazole)* Geodon (ziprasidone)*, ** Latuda (lurasidone)*,** Risperdal (risperidone) Saphris (asenapine) Seroquel (quetiapine) Zyprexa (olanzapine)	Common: increased appetite, weight gain, sedation, dizziness, dry mouth, blurred vision, muscle spasms, diabetes, restlessness, tremor Rare: tardive dyskinesia (repetitive, involuntary movements)

*do not have diabetes as a side effect; **do not cause increased appetite or weight gain
Note. From *Anxiety-Free Kids* (2nd ed., pp. 26–27), by B. Zucker, 2017, New York, NY: Routledge. Copyright 2017 by B. Zucker. Reprinted with permission of Routledge.

still need the standard CBT (E/RP) treatment, and may also be prescribed SSRIs. In addition, they may need antibiotics, immune therapies such as IVIG, steroids, or a tonsillectomy. Treatment protocols for PANDAS/PANS are still being researched.

Special Cases: When More Intensive Treatment Is Needed

As explained, not all OCD cases are the same. Some children and teens will require additional treatment, such as day treatment programs or inpatient hospitalizations. The Resources section in the back, as well as the IOCDF website, provides a list of hospital programs for OCD. The programs themselves have a screening process to assess if the child's OCD is severe enough to warrant hospitalization. Prior to going inpatient, most children will try outpatient therapy, and this can be increased to 2–3 times a week in the beginning if needed (typically, outpatient sessions are once a week). Usually, parents will have their child in therapy and on medication before considering if more intensive treatment is needed.

Although all children with OCD have symptoms that interfere in their daily life, most can still leave the house, attend school, and socialize to some extent. When you have a child who cannot leave the house or attend school and has completely isolated from peers, an inpatient or day treatment OCD-focused program can offer incredible hope. These intensive programs often result in rapid progress. I have had clients who have stayed for 2 weeks inpatient (usually followed by 1–2 weeks of day treatment at the same program, which is often for 10–12 hours a day), and it has resulted in life-changing progress. Then they return to outpatient therapy to continue the work and sustain the progress. Although it can be challenging to have your child or teen require hospitalization, it can also be relieving, as this likely means significant progress will be made in less time. Also, keep in mind that he will be with other children with an intense presentation of OCD, which can be both assuring and helpful (e.g., he won't feel alone, he may develop a better understanding of OCD, he can gain strength from seeing others make progress). If your child does participate in an inpatient day treatment (also called partial-hospitalization) program, it should *only* be an OCD-specific program. Otherwise, you risk having him receive ineffective treatment that only reinforces a sense of hopelessness. (My motto is that "no therapy is better than bad therapy," because the idea of being in therapy but not getting better creates this experience of hopelessness, for the child and the family. In other words, "We're getting help and doing what we are supposed to be doing, yet it's not getting better" is worse than "We haven't gotten the help we need yet," as the latter reflects that there is hope.)

In summary, finding the right therapist (and possibly psychiatrist) is the first step. Sometimes you might have to wait to get in with the right therapist; in the meantime, you can refer to Chapter 4 for some ideas of what to start doing (e.g., making self-talk cards, creating loop recordings, generating a list for the ladder). The next chapter will guide you on how you can best support your child, including how you can gradually stop the accommodations and strategies for collaborating with your child's school.

Chapter 6

Supporting Your Child's Treatment

There is a chapter in the *The OCD Workbook* (Hyman & Pedrick, 2010) called "OCD is a Family Affair," and that couldn't be any more accurate. OCD shapes your child's behavior, and therefore, it impacts you—the parents—and the home environment. Often, it impacts relationships with extended family and the child's experience at school and socially. As mentioned, family accommodations play a key role in the child's OCD experience, as parents get roped in and typically become a part of the neutralizing rituals.

When it comes to supporting your child's treatment at home, there are two phases: The first is how to help her before she has received CBT treatment, and the second is how to support her once she is receiving treatment. Ideally, your child's therapist will help guide you and give you specific strategies to use while your child is challenging her OCD. These phases speak to the likelihood that you will not abruptly discontinue the accommodations; rather, you will gradually reduce them as your child progresses through E/RP.

DOI: 10.4324/9781003237044-7

Tips for Supporting Your Child:
Prior to Beginning Treatment

What happens when you are trying to get everyone out the door in the morning and your child with OCD is stuck on taking his socks on and off over and over again, until the bottoms are aligned and "feel right"? The repeating behavior is causing a delay, and everyone may be late for school. What happens when this occurs on a morning in which you started out waking up late and have less time? It is in these moments when parents (understandably) lose their cool and can react negatively to their child's struggle. Even parents without OCD in their home can find themselves yelling and getting frustrated with delays in routine. When it comes to OCD, you have to start with acknowledging that *every day has built-in obstacles*. These built-in obstacles must be anticipated, planned for, and worked through. First and most important, you have to center yourself and empathize with your child's struggle. Using the socks example, can you imagine how incredibly frustrating and unsettling it must be to not be able to get your socks to feel right on your feet? For them to not look the right way or feel the right way, and all you want them to do is to be even and the same as each other, and yet you cannot get it right? Start with empathy! When you express empathy, and show that you get it, then your child knows that you are "with him," and this supports the team approach that is needed for this to work effectively. A comment such as, "Are you trying to get your socks to feel right? You must feel so frustrated right now," can take you far. Once your child has the language of OCD and understands the triggers, you can add: "Honey, I think your OCD has been set off" or "I think you are OCDing."

Once you have communicated empathy, you can then work on problem solving. Before he has received treatment, your objective is literally just to get through the trigger, and this will naturally require some accommodation. You can encourage him to take the socks off and calm down for a minute to interrupt the ritual and get his focus to shift onto something else. This alone can help reset him; however, many times you will not be able to get him to stop the behavior at all (e.g., he is trapped in the cycle of doing it over and over, with the typical tunnel vision that makes "getting it right" a prerequisite to doing anything else). The next option is to negotiate with the ritual. In this example, you can ask him to set a time limit on how many more minutes he will try to get the socks right before you give up and find another alternative (different socks, no socks, wear shoes that don't necessarily need socks, such as Crocs or Ugg-like shoes). By working with him in this way, you are acknowledging his struggle but are also reinforcing the idea that he has to stop the cycle at some point in order to function and proceed with the day. Also, by approaching it with empathy and problem solving in a collaborative way, you will avoid the power struggle and blow-up argument that this situation can often result in. If you know that socks are a daily struggle for him, be proactive and plan ahead the night before by talking with him about the time it takes and that you have some ideas to go over with him. Offer to set a time limit for say, 3 minutes, and if at the end of the time he still hasn't found a way to wear his socks, then he needs to come up with an alternative (e.g., no socks). I know that this socks example is overly simplistic and that your child may take 2 hours to get dressed and may never be "ready" to walk out the door, but it is useful for illustrating how the process works.

When you can anticipate a trigger, you have a head start on planning how your child will get through it. The harder challenge occurs when something unexpected triggers him and he becomes set off into the cycle of OCD; because there is no "convenient" time to be disrupted by OCD behaviors, you have to be prepared for these times by rehearsing in your head that you will (1) start with empathy and then (2) problem solve collaboratively with your child in the moment. It also goes a long way for you to plan and anticipate that triggers will happen suddenly, that you won't always understand why the trigger is a trigger for him, and that it will cause an interference in your day. Before you move into formal therapy, you want to join your child and help him navigate his way through the triggers. To summarize, until the OCD is treated: empathy FIRST, problem solve second. At this phase, the problem solving will involve accommodations on your part.

Accommodations

In terms of accommodations, even when your child is not yet receiving treatment, you want to work on scaling back on what you are doing in service of her OCD. All parents of children with anxiety end up accommodating it, and therefore unintentionally reinforcing, or strengthening it. With OCD, the tendency to accommodate is ever greater. And the accommodations lead to more family stress and worse OCD for the child. It's worth repeating that although parents and other family members make accommodations out of love, warmth, and compassion (and usually a bit of desperation), it makes the OCD stronger and results in a worsening of symptoms. When you provide the requested reassurance (e.g., when you answer "no" to her question "Will I get sick from touching that?"), it gives more power to the OCD and OCD thoughts that breed doubt. Essentially, if you are expending time and effort to answer the question, it gives validity to the question. Similarly, if you are spending so much time helping her clean a surface repeatedly, redo hair over and over, or check something 10 times to be sure it won't cause a fire, it strengthens her already-strong thought that these things are necessary and reasonable to do. Reassurance and participation in the rituals validates the OCD and makes your child's OCD worse, even though in the moment, it makes her feel better and relieves her distress. In the moment, it leads to relief but, again, this is short-term relief only (and long-term OCD).

Phasing out the accommodations will require you, the parent, to tolerate the discomfort in your child that comes from not doing the accommodations. When you don't do the accommodation or provide the reassurance, your child's anxiety will increase, and this is where you need to tolerate her discomfort (this will be particularly true during the E/RP work). Although parents do not cause anxiety, the way they respond to it can influence it, in good or bad ways. Any scaling back or limiting of the accommodations you make will benefit your child. I recommend that you share that you are reading this book and are learning about how accommodating the OCD only makes it worse and leads to more stress for the child and for the family. Explain that you will be working with her to minimize or reduce some of the accommodations that you (and other family members) have been doing, and that you will be there for her to help manage the discomfort. You can still support her emotionally, but not give into her requests or demands to accommodate. Using the getting dressed example, let's say that the ritual is for your daughter to have completely smooth hair in a pony-tail, and you accommodate by spending 45 minutes doing her hair, taking it in and out of the ponytail until it is "perfect" and smooth. You would start by having a discussion about how this is an OCD ritual and that you need to start to decrease the time you devote to this ritual: "So let's keep track for 3 days to see how long it's taking us, and then on the fourth day, I'm going to reduce the time that I'm available to help you with your hair by 10 minutes (or 20% of whatever time it is taking)." This is a great way to start reducing your participation in the OCD. It's not an abrupt change, but more of a gradual, planned one. This scaling back should be slow but steady: Pick two reasonably manageable changes to make and then a few days later, add a few more. If your child gets activated or overwhelmed, you can stay at the level of accommodation for a few more days, but then start to scale back again. Most importantly, try not to regress and go back to doing the accommodations you already gave up. For example, let's say that you reduced the time you were willing to devote to getting her hair "right" to 10 minutes. Even if one day, she gets incredibly distressed and wants you to spend more time, try to resist this. Explain that you have 10 minutes and no more than 10 minutes, and that's the only amount of time you are willing to serve the OCD. Point out that she was able to do it in 10 minutes yesterday (always cite previous progress whenever possible), and can do it again in 10 minutes today. Increasing it to 15 minutes will only cause a regression, and realistically your efforts won't lead to getting her hair "right." OCD can be relentless and becomes the priority for your child, taking so much time from her life. If you join in this, then the OCD is in control. Your resistance is the way you are taking back control of your life, and your child's.

Tips for Supporting Your Child: Once Treatment Has Begun

The second phase, when your child is receiving treatment for the OCD, involves a greater push to completely stop the accommodations.

Once your child is in treatment, the goal is to completely discontinue the accommodations and any participation in your child's rituals. Essentially, your child cannot overcome OCD unless you and other family members stop serving it by doing the accommodations. Being firm and unwilling to accommodate should be easier for you because your child will have support from her therapist and will have learned numerous strategies for dealing with the OCD (tools in her toolbox). It's also helpful to remind yourself that making all of these accommodations and assisting her with the rituals has not been an effective approach to dealing with the OCD: It has only served to maintain or worsen the OCD. You must take a new approach: You want to transition from doing the accommodations to creating an environment at home that is consistent with E/RP. Instead of accommodating, avoiding, and providing reassurance, your actions and reactions will now be in support of the E/RP approach. In the second phase, the plan will be clearer for you because: (1) you will receive guidance from the therapist, and (2) you will be more willing to stop the accommodations because you know your child is receiving outside support and also learning strategies to overcome the OCD. You will be guided by the ladder steps (using the hair example above, steps on the ladder would be "Mom spends no more than 2 minutes putting your hair in a ponytail," and "Do your hair on your own"), which require you to not participate.

When it comes to slowing down, minimizing, and stopping the accommodations all together, you need to know what to do instead. It's not just about stopping it; it's about replacing the accommodations with a more helpful approach, one that keeps you connected with your child and positions you to help support her in fighting the OCD. Here are some ideal responses that you can use in the moments when your child is triggered. Instead of engaging with the OCD, you will engage more directly with your child's struggle to fight it:

✧ I can see how hard this is for you. I know you are struggling. But I also know you can work through the OCD.

✧ Even though it may not feel like it, you can handle this.

✧ Remember, it's supposed to be hard when you don't give in. But stay with it and it will soon get better. The urge (or the anxiety) will lessen and eventually goes away.

✧ I know you want me to answer your questions, but I can't talk to the OCD. I can talk to you, but not the OCD.

✧ If you do the ritual, you will feel better, but the OCD will get worse. You have to deal with not feeling better right now and wait it out. This is how you fight the OCD. This is how *you* get stronger and it gets weaker.

✧ You were able to do this before, so you have it in you do to it again.

✧ It's only the OCD talking. Stamp the thought! Stamp it "OCD"!

✧ I see you're really having a hard time. Let's take a moment and try to calm your body. Let's do the one-nostril breathing.

✧ You'll never feel "ready" to do this—you just have to force yourself to deal with the discomfort, which starts out worse and will soon get better.

✧ Think about what someone without OCD would think. What would they do?

✧ Be proactive and let your values guide you. Your decisions need to be in support of fighting the OCD.

Because your refusal to participate in the OCD will increase anxiety in your child, things will become more intense, temporarily. Keep the word *temporary* in your mind, because it will allow you to have a greater range of what you can tolerate in terms of distress in your child. You have to *temporarily* get through the discomfort in order to come out on the other side. Dealing with OCD in your child is always an emotional experience, but when you are doing the E/RP work and eventually refusing to participate in her OCD, the emotionality will increase. It is essential that you manage your own reactions (frustration, anxiety, helplessness) when helping your child in the E/RP challenges. If you respond to her struggle with frustration and anger, it will make it worse. Think about it: We know that stress makes OCD worse, so the more stressful the environment (even if that stress comes in reaction to the OCD behaviors), the more stuck the child will feel. Her OCD symptoms will get worse, and she will feel even more committed to doing the rituals to try to experience a sense of relief. If she is stuck in putting her socks on and off over and over, she is already activated; if her parent starts yelling and screaming at her for doing this and for being late, and so on, she will become even more attached to doing the ritual to seek the relief that comes from getting her socks on the right way. I truly get how parents feel this way—the behavior is nonsensical, redundant, and can feel maddening to witness—yet these feelings need to be dealt with and managed effectively and cannot become part of the child's experience with OCD. Instead, you want the struggle to be between her and the OCD (not her and you); let the process of facing her fears unfold for her, and make yourself in the background as a loving and supportive, yet strong in your commitment to not do any accommodations, parent. Basically, stay as calm as possible and keep some distance between you and her OCD; be a bit detached from her process of OCD. The goal is to stay connected with and be supportive of her, but not the OCD.

Parenting Styles

The best parenting style is the "authoritative" one, which is when a parent has high warmth and high demand (Baumrind, 1971). Authoritative parents show empathy and warmth yet do not compromise on their values or give into the child's anxiety. For example, if an anxious child doesn't want to go to school, the authoritative parent would respond with, "I understand you don't want to go, and it's making you feel anxious, but you cannot miss school—you know you have to go." The other types—permissive and authoritarian—are commonly seen in parents of children with OCD and anxiety. The permissive type has high warmth and low demand ("I know how hard this is for you; you can stay home today"), whereas the authoritarian type has low warmth and high demand ("I don't care how you feel . . . you are going to school"). Many times you will have one parent who is permissive and one parent who is authoritarian. The permissive parent sees the authoritarian parent as harsh and cold, and the authoritarian parent sees the permissive parent as weak and too soft; when this combo happens (which is common), they each become stronger in their parenting style in response to the other's approach. The good news is, when working with parents who have this combo, I inform them that they are both using the wrong style! The permissive parent needs to have more demand, and the authoritarian parent needs to have more warmth. You cannot just have one; you have to have both. You must become an authoritative parent! In a two-parent family with a child with OCD, both parents need to adopt the same style of authoritative parenting. This is the parenting style that you can have confidence in, as it is the best style and approach for parenting a child with OCD.

Fundamentally, authoritative parents rely on their values, not their feelings, when making parenting decisions, including those pertaining to the OCD. Using values as a guide for decisions is the same as being proactive and, as explained in Chapter 4, we want your child to be proactive as well. Therefore, when you learn to be proactive, this is a good model for the child. In fact, you can point out that by not giving into the OCD by making accommodations, you are modeling for him to not give in as well.

In summary, the difference between the two phases (before treatment and during treatment) is about your willingness to accommodate the OCD. Also, once your child is in treatment, you will still give empathy and problem solve, but most of your involvement will be to cue him to use his strategies and fight back against the OCD.

During both phases (before treatment, during treatment), it is essential that you are positive and encouraging, and also reinforcing the right messages to promote a sense of resilience in your child. Resilience is not letting obstacles stand in our way and having the belief that no matter what comes our way, we can handle it. OCD presents a huge obstacle in your child's life, and knowing that he can face his fears (through E/RP) and overcome it offers a most meaningful opportunity to become resilient. You can help him with this by framing the OCD as a challenge to be overcome (rather than a "why me?" approach, which only serves to make your child feel disempowered and like a victim). We cannot control the fact that your child developed OCD, but we can control the outcome. Knowing that one can control the outcome in his life is referenced as having an *internal locus of control*. Someone with an internal locus of control has self-efficacy and believes that he can affect his experience in life—he can change the outcome. The opposite of this is an *external locus of control*, which is when the control is outside of the person; no matter what he does, he can't change the situation. We want to encourage an internal locus of control: Even if in the moment we cannot impact the situation directly (the outcome may sometimes not be that different even with this mindset), we can still change our experience of the situation. By thinking a different way and adopting a positive attitude, we can get through it and not be that impacted. What we tell ourselves during the rough times in life has an enormous influence in how those rough times are experienced. You can watch two people going through the same obstacle, with two totally different experiences and two different long-term outcomes as a result.

Siblings and Family Members

Siblings and others in the home will also feel the impact of the OCD. It is important for siblings to have purposeful one-on-one time with each parent to help them process what it is like for them to have a sibling with OCD. Interestingly, the same approach of empathy first, problem solve second, works with your other children as well. Validate what it is like for them, how much time and energy the sibling with OCD takes and requires of you. Normalize the fact that sometimes in a family, one member needs more tending to, and that this is only temporary. Empathize with what it feels like to be in a family where a member has a diagnosable psychological problem; ensure that they know it is treatable and that many families have a member with an anxiety disorder. Then work with the non-OCD child on problem solving; for example, develop a plan so the non-OCD child is not late for school because of his sibling's OCD and knows what can he do if he is in a public place when his sibling is triggered. Problem solving at the specific level can go a long way in helping your other child feel that he has a plan to cope. He also might require guidance from you when it comes to what he should say and do in response to the OCD and specifically, what happens when he gets roped into the symptoms or ends up participating in accommodations. Assuming he is old enough (older sibling of at least 10 years old), your other child needs to be trained to respond in the same way you do to the reassurance-seeking and request for accommodations; he, too, needs to scale back and ultimately eliminate the accommodations, and he needs to learn what to say instead. In the next chapter, we will go through case examples, including a few in which siblings were included in the treatment process.

Similarly, extended family, especially those living in close proximity, may require some psychoeducation about OCD and your child's symptoms. They may need to be coached on how to respond, including what to say to support your child and not shame her in any way. Many times, extended family will be able to identify another relative with OCD, and sometimes that OCD was untreated or the person has suffered for years without effective treatment. It is essential that you draw a distinction between that person and your child who is receiving empirically supported treatment (CBT) and as a result, will have a different (better) outcome. The goal is to ensure that your child is not overly pathologized by well-meaning relatives.

Social Implications

When it comes to your child's social experience, OCD can cause an interference in several ways. Practically, your child may miss social events or social opportunities because the OCD symptoms prevent her from leaving the house or getting to the event on time, or the event itself could be a trigger. For example, a sleepover party might put her at greater risk for getting sick (contamination type). Going to a movie with friends may elicit her fear of seeing "inappropriate" (sexual) content. Being near a swimming pool may trigger her urge to ensure that no one runs or slips and also her desire to keep surfaces dry and safe. Any social situation that is avoided should be integrated into the ladder. She may decide to open up to one or two friends about her OCD, and this can make engaging in social events more likely because it offers a bit of a crutch (which is fine in the beginning if it encourages her participation). Although most friends will be supportive and kind, some may not respond as favorably. Some children will not know what to say in support (e.g., some may ask a lot of question, that cause your child to be uncomfortable), or others may pass judgment and distance themselves. Ideally, you can help your child select which friend(s) to tell, and you can prepare your child for how it might be received and what to say in response if it doesn't go well. For example, if a friend doesn't know what to say in response to your child's disclosure, you can prepare your child on how to move the conversation on to another topic. Role-playing what to say in response, including how to be assertive if someone acts in a judgmental way (e.g., "I was hoping that you'd be understanding, but I see that's hard for you. Let's talk about [or play] something else."), will allow your child to feel more confident about disclosing to others. The overarching goal is to help your child get her social needs met. The more connected she feels, the better off she will be.

Teachers may have a hard time with being understanding or granting extra time when it is warranted; this is largely due to a lack of awareness of OCD and, specifically, how it affects the child. For this reason, you or your child's therapist may need to advocate for your child's rights in school (to get accommodations such as extra time when necessary). Note that these types of accommodations are entirely different from familial accommodations that involve participation in rituals, etc. Teachers (and other school faculty such as the school counselor) should be told about the OCD diagnosis when the symptoms are interfering with the child's participation in class. Explaining the cycle of OCD is a great place to start. Then give examples of what triggers are coming up in school. For example, a child with OCD who is leaving class several times during the day to use the bathroom may be misunderstood to be a behavior problem (someone who doesn't want to stay in class or do the work), and it is important to clarify the urges, compulsions, and so on.

Without giving every detail or compromising your child's privacy, providing a few examples of how it manifests in school is necessary for both preventing your child from being punished (penalized) for OCD symptoms at school and for helping her work toward overcoming the OCD (it is useful for your child's school environment to give the same messages as she receives at home regarding facing her fears or delaying the rituals, etc.). Regarding the latter, in an ideal situation, the school counselor and teacher can be trained to cue the child to use her strategies while in school. Your child should know that the teacher(s) and school counselor understand OCD and are there to help her, and that they know she is working hard to overcome OCD. A teacher can cue by saying something privately (in a whisper) to the child about limiting bathroom trips: "I know you feel like you want to go right now to wash your hands, but can you try to hold off for 5 more minutes?" For the child who keeps writing and erasing and rewriting over and over, the teacher could say, "Let's take a break from this and work on something else for a bit." A school counselor could be available to do some calm breathing or do a quick "stamping it OCD" exercise for the child who is really activated and anxious at school. This kind of support can go a long way in helping your child. However, some kids may feel embarrassed or shamed by this, and if that happens, then the teacher should not be as direct, although the school counselor should always make her- or himself available when possible. When the environments at home, at school, and with extended family and close friends are in sync in that they encourage facing the OCD and fighting the urges, your child will benefit enormously and receive the support he needs to see the OCD as OCD and do the work involved with fighting it. I have had teenage clients who have shared about their OCD with close, loving friends who have actually cued them to use their strategies ("Read your cards; you don't need to wash") or provided a reality-check ("You're OCD-ing; you don't need to keep checking with me, it's fine). Although this is not the norm, it is a good example of how the environment can support your child in the struggle to overcome OCD.

Parental Modeling

Finally, modeling healthy behaviors can help your child gauge what is appropriate, for example, when it comes to handwashing, cleaning, being thorough, etc. Siblings, too, can be helpful in modeling non-OCD behavior for everyday kinds of things. For example, a sibling may put her homework in her backpack and then go up to bed, showing her sibling with OCD what is reasonable in terms of being prepared (whereas the child with OCD may check six times to make sure his homework is in his backpack). However, this needs to be done in a gentle, nonshaming manner. If you are a parent with OCD, then you can explain to your child that you are not the best model for hand-washing, but that _____(fill in the blank with someone who is) is a good guidepost. Helping your child to find the right balance by stating rules with confidence ("We wash hands after the bathroom, and sometimes before meals and sometimes after meals when we are messy.") is beneficial.

Chapter 7

Case Examples

Bringing It All Together

In this chapter, we will go through 10 case examples (names and identifying characteristics have been changed), including typical and atypical presentations of OCD. Most of these examples were introduced in Chapter 2. In each example, we will look at the symptoms and the treatment plan, including family involvement. The following is a summary of the 10 examples:

Case 1: Jaxon, age 9, Contamination type

Case 2: Desiree, age 16, Contamination type

Case 3: Jared, age 15, Contamination type

Case 4: Casey, age 10, Fear of Doing Harm/Overresponsibility type

Case 5: Nico, age 13, Doubting/Indecisive type

Case 6: Sean, age 11, Symmetry/Just Feels Right type

Case 7: Ashley, age 12, Need to Confess type

Case 8: Chris, age 14, Scrupulosity type

Case 9: Ana, age 12, Scrupulosity type

Case 10: Kaitlyn, age 8, "Bad" Thoughts type

 DOI: 10.4324/9781003237044-8

Most cases follow a similar course of treatment. Beginning with an intake assessment, I learn about the child's symptoms and OCD presentation, trying to gather as many specific examples as possible (in fact, on a separate sheet of paper, I often start writing the list of items that will be used for the ladder). I also find out how the family reacts to or accommodates the child's OCD, as this is an important part of the therapy. Once the intake is completed, I teach the OCD cycle, three parts of anxiety, calm breathing, and one-nostril breathing. In the second–fifth sessions, I explain the bulk of the strategies and make self-talk cards, create the ladder, have the child record the loop and uncertainty recordings, and teach detached mindfulness. During this time, I also ensure that the child has a clear understanding of his OCD and the plan we are going to follow to overcome it. My goal is to start the exposures by the sixth session, but I explain that we will go at a comfortable pace for him. I am encouraging and positive about doing the exposures and order them from easiest to hardest. As previously stated, we can always break a step down into smaller steps. Even for severe cases, the client and I work together to find even a small part of an easier step that he is willing to work on or for me to model for him first. I firmly believe that the theme of "we need to fight the OCD" should be honored from the start of the treatment, so the sooner we start exposures, the better (and, again, these can be super small steps in the beginning). I find it very helpful to have a structure to the therapy, particularly for children with anxiety and OCD. OCD and anxiety can make a child feel so consumed with discomfort and fear; many kids feel uneasy about this, and the whole thing can feel chaotic and ungrounding. With a clear and organized approach to treating the OCD, the child begins to feel hopeful and can feel a bit at ease; also, as he progresses in learning the strategies and starting to do the exposures, his confidence builds. It is this confidence that ultimately leads him to overcome the OCD!

Case 1: Jaxon, Age 9, Contamination Type

Description of Jaxon's OCD

Around third grade, Jaxon started to have a hard time touching things because of germs. After learning in school about health and how important frequent handwashing is to avoid getting the flu and other illness, he began to avoid touching doorknobs, cabinet door handles, faucet handles, and other shared surfaces. He washed his hands multiple times throughout the day. His mother was vigilant about washing hands each time they came in from the house and before they would eat. She carried antibacterial wipes with her, and before they sat at a table when eating out (for example, at the mall food court), she sanitized the table, the edges, and the seats. He always felt better when she was there to make it clean. At lunch at school, he would lay paper towels under his lunch bag and anywhere he put his food. His friends started to ask him about his behavior and were clearly noticing that he was anxious. His worry about coming in contact with germs ("getting germs on me," as he would say) started to get out of control, and the handwashing, cleaning of surfaces, and worry itself was taking more and more time every day. He decided to keep certain clothes clean from the outside by not wearing them out of the house, and would change into these clothes when he came in. His mother did the same, so when they came into the house, they would leave most of their clothes in the mudroom and would have clean pajamas to change into (already laid out in advance). When his dad came home, Jaxon would ask him to change, but Dad refused, which made him upset. Dad did agree, however, to not sit on Jaxon's bed with his "outside" clothes and also to not wear his shoes in the house. If Dad took him to eat out and Mom wasn't there, Dad would not clean the table off (he told Jaxon "the table was already clean"), and Jaxon would get upset and wipe down his part of the table with water and some napkins. He asked his mom to talk with his dad about bringing the antibacterial wipes with him. Dad was worried about how much focus germs had become for Jaxon, and Mom agreed that it was too much of a focus for him (and for her also).

Mom's friend had a daughter who went to therapy for her anxiety, and it seemed to be working, so she asked her for the name of the therapist.

Jaxon came in with both Mom and Dad, who were clearly very warm and invested parents. We discussed how he met the criteria for OCD because his symptoms (obsessions and compulsions) were taking an hour or more a day and caused an interference in his life. We discussed how his mother, who was a self-described "germ-o-phobe," would need to learn how to challenge her own behavior (which we discussed was excessive on its own but, more importantly, supported and reinforced Jaxon's OCD). We also discussed how his father would have to be more patient, and, although he was the one with a more "normal" approach to cleanliness, we wanted him to be a bit more collaborative with Jaxon and not just insist on doing it his way. Both parents were receptive to this guidance.

Treatment of Jaxon's OCD

As with all cases of OCD, I started with an explanation of the three parts of anxiety (body, thoughts, and behavior) and the OCD cycle. We went through his cycle:

1. Event: Touch doorknob while walking into class.
2. Thought/Urge: What if I have germs on me now?
3. Feeling: Anxious, unclean, dirty, disgusted.
4. Action/Ritual: Wash hands with soap and warm water in classroom sink before sitting down at desk.

We went through another two examples of his OCD cycle:

1. Go to dinner at restaurant.
2. This table could be very dirty and germy; many people have sat here.
3. Anxious, uncomfortable.
4. Sanitize table, table edges, and seats before sitting down at table; wash hands before and after meal.

1. Walking into the house.
2. These clothes are dirty—there are probably so many germs all over them. If I sit on the couch with these or go into my room, the couch and my room will become dirty and germy, and I will get the germs on me during my sleep.
3. Anxious.
4. Change into clean pajamas and wear those inside house instead.

Seeing the cycle helped Jaxon to better understand how his everyday experience was the expression of OCD. He learned about the connection between the event-thought-feeling behavior. When viewed this way, the behavior that feels so necessary and logical at the time is more accurately understood as part of the OCD symptoms. Therefore, the value of going though the cycle is to promote understanding, as it did for Jaxon.

I explained and had him practice calm breathing and one-nostril breathing. Jaxon really liked learning progressive muscle relaxation; he benefitted from a recording I made in which a wave comes over your body and relaxes all of your muscles. Then, when it goes down and leaves your body, it takes with it all of the tension and stress. We also liked the Calm app. I made Jaxon many self-talk cards, and he identified three favorites: "What would someone without OCD do in this situation?", "Other kids touch doorknobs without thinking about it," and "Once I prevent a ritual, it will get easier. It's just hard at first and then I will get used to it." They took pictures of these cards on both Mom's and Dad's phones so he could read them when they were in situations in which he was going to face his fears, like eating out. We also went through the thinking errors, and explained how he was using all-or-nothing thinking and catastrophizing, and generated replacement thoughts such as "It's okay to wear these clothes inside the house, like most people do, and doing that doesn't mean I'm going to get sick" and "Being healthy has lots of parts to it—I take good care of my body, and my body is strong." He also thought a lot about what other people do and how most people do not change when they get home, so he backed up these replacement thoughts with good information to consider.

We also recorded a loop and uncertainty training recording from this typed script:

What if I get germs on me? What if I get flu germs on me and get the flu? What if I get sick? What if I touch the faucet and get germs on me? I need to wash my hands. I need to wash my hands again. I need mom to clean the table. What if we don't clean the table and we touch germs or germs get in our food? Then we will really get sick! What if germs get in my food at lunch?

It is always possible that germs will get on me. It's possible that I will get flu germs on me and get the flu. It's possible that I will get sick. It's always possible that I will touch the faucet and get germs on me. It's always possible that we won't clean the table and will touch germs and that germs will get in our food and we will get really sick. It's possible that germs will get in my food at lunch.

Jaxon listened to this recording, which was on the shorter side (about 1 minute) 10 times every day for 2 weeks. Although the first 3 days he listened brought a rise in his anxiety, by the end of the second week, he said he was "so bored" hearing these thoughts and that they did nothing to him at all. He also noted that he had hardly any of these thoughts during the day anymore. Jaxon responded very well to the loop recording. He also did an incredible job at facing his fears, using the ladder below (harder items on the top, easier items on the bottom):

(top)	Wear outside pants under the covers.
	Wear outside pants and sit on bed.
	Mom and Dad wear outside pants under covers.
	Mom sits on bed with outside pants.
	Dad sits on bed with outside pants.
	Sit on edge of bed with outside pants.
	Wear outside clothes in bedroom.

Wear outside shorts and pants inside.
Wear outside pants and change shirt.
Wear outside shirt inside and change pants.
Eat chips from floor at grocery store.
Eat sample foods at grocery store (from back, from front, crumb pieces).
Eat chips from floor in Bonnie's office.
Eat lunch at school; food touches table and you still eat it.
Eat lunch at school; let fork touch table and eat with fork.
Eat lunch at school, no paper towels.
Go to restaurant with Mom and eat at unclean table, no wipes.
Go to coffee shop with Mom and sit at unclean table, no wipes.
Go to lunch with Mom and Dad—no sanitizing, no wipes.
Go to lunch with Mom—light cleaning of table, no wipes.
Go to lunch with Mom—light cleaning of table (not edges, not seats, with wipes).
Go to lunch with Dad—light cleaning of table.
Touch faucet handles, then eat apple slices without washing first.
Touch doorknob, then eat pretzels without washing first.
Touch faucet handles without rewashing.
Touch cabinet doorknobs.
Touch doorknobs without washing (1, 3, 5, 10 minutes . . . not until next meal or bathroom).

| (bottom) | Shake hands with someone who has touched doorknobs. |

Many people without OCD may not wear outside clothes under their bed covers or eat food from the floor, and without context, some of these ladder items may seem a bit over the top. However, to overcome OCD, the person needs to be exposed to more extreme practices, as research shows that doing this leads to greater improvement. Jaxon navigated through his ladder quite well. As much as possible, we did the practices together, and then he followed up with practicing on his own over the week. Also, I did many of the items first (and often in a more dramatic way) to model for him. For example, we went to Starbucks together and sat at an unclean table, and I ate a scone (including crumbs) directly from the table. Seeing me do this with ease was helpful; I also told him that I do this kind of thing almost daily and rarely get sick! This kind of reassurance was useful for the beginning of our work together; as we advanced in the ladder and went back to Starbucks for a similar practice, we commented, "It's always possible we'll get sick from this," and "Lots of people have been sick with the flu, and probably many of them come to eat at this Starbucks." These comments helped to further challenge the OCD and gain power over it—sort of like an *I don't care what you say, OCD, I'm going to eat from this table AND talk about the flu!* Like most kids, Jaxon found it somewhat amusing to be given so much freedom to talk back to the OCD in this way.

In my work with Jaxon, I had two parent sessions to help prepare his mother and father for the exposures. They brought his folder with them, and we reviewed the self-talk cards for them to use to cue Jaxon during exposures. I gave them a list of parental responses so they would know exactly what to say when he asked for accommodations or reassurance. We spoke about Mom's own germ issues, and I explained that while they were extreme, they didn't cause any real interference in her life; however, her germ issues were supporting Jaxon's OCD, which was a problem for him and did cause an interference in his life. We also discussed how she was not a "germ-o-phobe" as a child (it began when she became an adult, particularly once she had children), so it wasn't a part of her identity development as it was for Jaxon. It was a challenge for her to do some of the exposures on his ladder, so I recommended she do the practices by herself first. Dad was on board, learned how to be more flexible in the beginning, and was better able to meet Jaxon where he was.

Within 4 months, Jaxon had made significant progress in overcoming his OCD, and we slowed down to every other week. Three months later, he graduated from therapy. He worked very hard for these results; he put 100% in and got 100% out, as did his parents, who diligently ensured that he did his practices and were part of the process with him. Jaxon's OCD was fairly straightforward, as was his treatment process.

Case 2: Desiree, Age 16, Contamination Type

Description of Desiree's OCD

Desiree's OCD was about getting sick and throwing up. She worried about choking on her food or choking from vomiting. Winter was the worst time of the year for her because so many people get sick. She avoided places where there were lots of people, like the mall or the movies because she thought there was a good chance that most likely someone in the crowd would be sick. Desiree didn't like to go to any house party because there were so many kids in one small place. She got stomachaches all the time and worried that it was the beginning of the stomach bug and that she would throw up. When she was triggered by a stomachache, she would avoid sitting in the middle of anything, such as the inside of a booth, because if she needed to throw up, it would take longer to get out. She stayed away from other kids who had recently been sick or if someone in their family had been sick, particularly if it was with a stomach flu. She also used Purell and washed her hands frequently to prevent getting sick. Desiree refused to eat when she was the only one at home, as she was worried that she might choke and then no one would be there to save her. She became restrictive with the foods that she would eat; she stopped eating rice, pasta, granola bars, or anything sticky like Rice Krispies treats because she said they were hard to chew and digest. She also refused to eat anything that had ever been recalled; so she didn't eat red meat, spinach, pistachios, frozen vegetables, soft cheeses, or cucumbers. She checked the expiration dates before eating anything, especially dairy products. She wouldn't be the first person to drink from a carton of milk and would wait until the next day before drinking from it, to make sure that no one got sick from it. She also avoided eating leftovers because she heard that bacteria grew in the fridge. Desiree asked her parents if she could see a therapist to help with how anxious she felt. They had tried therapy when she was younger, and it wasn't very helpful (turns out, it was a therapist who took a more psychodynamic approach to trying to help with her anxiety); this time, they learned that CBT was the most helpful treatment for anxiety. They came to a talk I was giving at her school and then brought Desiree in for treatment.

Unlike most families with children with OCD, Desiree's family did little to accommodate her OCD. They typically challenged her beliefs about getting sick and often argued with her to not avoid any foods. If she asked someone in her family to drink from a new carton of milk, they would comply but simultaneously tell her that she was overreacting and that "it's just milk." They supported her therapy and were pleased that she was the one to initiate. They complimented her maturity and openness. In therapy, she was authentic and open about her symptoms and knew before coming in that she had anxiety. We discussed OCD, and I briefly explained why she met the criteria for diagnosis, which made sense to her.

Treatment of Desiree's OCD

After learning about the three parts of anxiety (body, thoughts, and behavior), we went through a few examples of her OCD cycle:

1. Event: Sitting next to a friend who tells you that her brother has stomach flu.
2. Thought/Urge: What if she has it also and now I'm going to get it? The stomach flu is so contagious!
3. Feeling: Anxious, restless.
4. Action/Ritual: Make an excuse to leave the situation. Stay away from friend for a few more days until it is clear she is not sick.

1. Feel hungry but I'm the only one at home.
2. What if I start choking when I'm eating and can't get it out and no one is here to help and I end up choking and die?
3. Anxious, panicky.
4. Call Mom and Dad to see if they are on their way, wait until someone gets home to eat.

She grasped the cycle and realized how so much of her behavior had been organized by the OCD. She commented, "I know it's crazy that I can't eat when no one is at home," demonstrating that she had good awareness of the OCD. I taught her calm breathing and relaxation, and she was a big fan of the Insight Timer app; she listened to a few of them with repetition and began to associate the tracks with calmness. We made many self-talk cards and did detached mindfulness as well. We discussed how she used "catastrophizing" and was constantly visualizing the worst-case scenario. We also did "stamping it OCD," which she really liked. When she was triggered, she wrote down all of her thoughts and wrote "OCD" using a red thick Sharpie over them, all of which were OCD thoughts. As she did this, she said, "It's OCD; it doesn't count. Not a real thought." Most of all, Desiree benefitted a great deal from listening to her loop recordings and explained that the uncertainty training component was particularly useful for her. Throughout the year-long therapy, she made about 10 loop recordings, many of which were focused on a theme (for example, choking while at home alone), and she elaborated on all of the thoughts she had surrounding that one trigger. Here is a sample script of one of her recordings:

I hate eating when no one is home. It's better just to starve. Even if I have to go to bed hungry, it's better than choking to death. I know that you can't talk when choking so even calling 911 wouldn't matter, plus I wouldn't be able to get to the phone on time. It would be so terrible if I died that way and then my parents would find me and it would be horrible. I think I have a narrow digestive track—it takes me too long to get the food down and I just think that can't be normal. Probably there is something abnormal about it and it will be discovered once I choke and die. Humans are so fragile. I could also throw up and choke that way. I know there are people who've died from choking on their vomit. It's always possible I will choke. It's always possible I will be alone and the food will get stuck and no one will be there to save me and then I will die. It's possible I will die from choking. It's always possible that I have something anatomically wrong that prevents the food from going down and gives me a higher chance of choking. It's always possible that I will throw up and choke on my throw up.

Desiree found making the loop recordings in this way—exactly as the thoughts sounded in her head and including all of the different thoughts she had—was the best way to challenge the OCD thoughts. She would sometimes listen to her recordings for 30–45 minutes a day. She learned how to habituate to her thoughts. She also made and listened to recordings that were specifically matched to the steps on the ladder (for example, she listened to the script above early in the day before she did the practices that were associated with eating while at home alone). Then, once she was doing the exposure, she used self-talk to help her cope with the anxiety in the moment.

We constructed her ladder; I made most of the suggestions based on her explanation of her symptoms.

(top)

Eat 3-day-old meat leftovers.
Eat 2-day-old meat leftovers.
Eat 1-day-old meat leftovers.
Eat "expired" yogurt.
Sit next to someone who had been sick with stomach flu.
Sit next to someone whose family member has had stomach flu recently.
Eat when no one is at home, parents are out for the night.
Eat when no one is at home, but they are on their way (10 minutes away).
Eat when no one is at home, but parents are on the phone and around the corner.
Eat when parents are outside in yard.
Eat food previously recalled.
Stop using Purell.
Eat yogurt without checking expiration date.
Drink milk without checking expiration date.
Be the first to drink from a carton of milk.
Eat foods from avoided list.
Eat meat from restaurant.
Eat meat from home.
Eat food hard to digest (rice, granola).
Go to the movies and sit in middle with a stomachache.
Sit in a booth when you have a stomachache.
Go to a house party (30 minutes, 1 hour, whole party).
Go to the movies and sit in the middle.
Go to the movies and sit on aisle seat.

(bottom)	Go to the mall.

Desiree and I did many of these exposures together. For example, we had one session at Chipotle, and she ate half of her steak burrito bowl. I took the leftovers to my office and then had her come the next day after school to eat the leftovers (for this appointment, I scheduled my lunch at the same time she came by, so I could do the exposure with her). We did the same thing for 2- and 3-day leftovers. When she ate while no one was at home, she started with "easy" foods and then moved to harder-to-digest trigger foods, such as rice and granola bars. She did the first half of the ladder with relative ease; when it came to eating alone, being near someone who was sick or had a family member who was sick, and eating meat leftovers, Desiree had to use a lot of her techniques (especially one-nostril breathing, which she used regularly), and those exposures took a lot longer for her to do. She broke the steps down into even smaller tasks; for example, when it came to eating the meat leftovers, she started with just a few bites at a time and then gradually increased the amount. Again, the goal is to make progress in the exposures; the pace is not as important. With each movement forward, Desiree gained momentum and was successful in completing her ladder.

After a year of weekly therapy, we slowed down to twice a month, then 6 months later, once a month. After 2 years, she went to college, and at that point, she stopped coming regularly, although she saw me for check-ins about three times a year when she was home. She maintained her progress throughout college and found the only time she had a return of any symptoms was during exam time, when she was very stressed. In her visits home, our work was focused on stress management, as there weren't any true OCD symptoms anymore.

Case 3: Jared, Age 15, Contamination Type

Description of Jared's OCD

Jared had always been on the anxious side and was a sensitive child. He used to be close to his younger sister, Rachel, but in the last few years they had grown apart. Starting in eighth grade, he began avoiding things she touched or was near. He wouldn't sit where she had sat, wouldn't share his food with her, and wouldn't let her in his room. He was also rude about it. By ninth grade, it was causing a big problem for everyone at home. Jared wouldn't use anything that Rachel had used, even if it was cleaned. He made a separate space for "his" dishes, glasses, and utensils that he washed himself and put back in the shelf. He cleaned anything she may have touched before he used it himself (for example, he cleaned the remote after she used it). He also declared his spot on the couch and his chair at the table and told his sister not to sit there. He had his mom and dad wash his clothes in a separate wash than his sister's; once when his dad "mixed" an outfit of his sister's in a wash with mostly his clothes, Jared washed his clothes a second time in a separate cycle. His sister was angry as a result of his behavior and mistreatment of her (he would yell and scream at her, constantly telling her to "get away from me"); she started screaming back at him, and they both stopped having friends over to the house if the other was there. Their parents were divorced but worked together well as coparents; his sister would arrange to have sleepovers only if Jared was at the other parent's house. Both parents were stuck in the middle, trying to make Jared comfortable, but also felt defensive of his sister. Plus, from a practical standpoint, it had become difficult and quite inconvenient. They decided it was time for him to get therapy.

Jared was initially resistant to coming to therapy. He felt that his sister was "really gross," was repulsed by her, and felt that he shouldn't have to be near her. His parents looked to me for guidance and were relieved when I told them that we were going to move in the direction of no longer accommodating his requests to not be at the same house as Rachel. When meeting with just his parents, they expressed concern that he would not cooperate with the therapy. I explained that in cases where the child refuses to change or work on it, we make the change at the family systems level; for example, if he refused to engage in the therapy process (beyond the normal resistance at the start), then we would let him know that his parents would have to change and would no longer accommodate his requests or preferences when it came to his sister. We discussed how decisions need to move from considering the OCD to reflecting their family values, which for them was to have both kids together at one of their homes. It went beyond inconvenience, as his parents really struggled with what felt like entitlement on Jared's part, and his unkind behavior toward his sister made them feel defensive. We discussed all of this together in an open manner at the intake appointment. They found it helpful when I framed it through the lens of OCD, taking into account Jared's age (15) and normalizing the egocentricism (seeing everything from one's own perspective) that is typical of the teenage years. Although Jared did not come in with any openness to the idea of getting closer in any way to his sister, he did agree to work on his attitude and agreed that being more flexible would make life easier for him and his family. Once we got into it, he actually did great and participated fully in the treatment.

Treatment of Jared's OCD:

We went through his OCD cycle:
1. Event: See Rachel in living room sitting on couch watching TV.
2. Thought/Urge: I can't go near her. I can't let her touch me.
3. Feeling: Anxious, disgusted.
4. Action/Ritual: Avoid living room and when she leaves, clean remote.

We discussed his irritability and the mind-body connection; he benefitted from understanding how relaxing his body could help his mind. I taught him relaxation, and despite his initial resistance, he began listening to Mooji's "Nothing Here But You" track on Insight Timer every night before bed. This taught him how to meditate. I also taught him several yoga poses to use—he liked downward dog and doing handstands against the wall. Then we worked on the thoughts component and discussed how he was using "all-or-nothing thinking" when it came to Rachel: He labeled her and everything she touched as contaminated. There was no middle ground or flexibility at all. We also discussed how he was using "emotional reasoning" to explain the situation: Because he felt disgusted by her, he assumed that she was actually a disgusting person. I made him a few self-talk cards. We did not do any loop recordings, as most of his anxiety was emotional (a feeling state), and he did not have many thoughts about his triggers. For Jared, the behavioral exposures were what led him to overcome his OCD. He used the following ladder to help.

(top)	Sleep in bed after Rachel slept there (no washing sheets).
	Sleep on pillow used by Rachel (no washing pillowcase).
	Eat from shared bowl with Rachel (share chips and salsa, share dessert).
	Eat food prepared by Rachel.
	Eat food handed to you by Rachel.
	Wash clothes with Rachel's clothes.
	Have Rachel come in your room (first with you there, then when you're not).
	Use utensils, glasses that were handwashed.
	Sit on Rachel's side of couch.
	Sit on Rachel's side of car.
	Sit on Rachel's chair.
	Use the remote after Rachel hands it to you.
	Go in Rachel's room.
	Show kindness to Rachel.

	Use utensils from both houses after cleaned in dishwasher.
	Use glasses from both houses after cleaned in dishwasher.
	Use plates from both houses after cleaned in dishwasher.
(bottom)	Touch items touched by Rachel.

Jared struggled with most of the items on his ladder. The main thing that got him through was telling himself that "there is no way out but through" and that if he "sat with" the discomfort, it would go away. After doing this a few times and seeing that the anxiety went away, he was able to do more and more exposures and grew in his confidence about the treatment plan. His parents were very supportive and encouraging. We did many of the exposures together: He brought in plates, glasses, and utensils from his houses, and he used them to eat in my office; his mom brought in a scarf, a book, and a tissue box all belonging to Rachel, and we worked together to have Jared touch each item and use a tissue. I went to his house twice to help him with sitting on her side of the couch and in her chair and also in her seat in the car, because he was not doing these exposures on his own (as a side note, Jared lived 15 minutes from my office and I did 30-minute sessions—instead of 50—so I could keep the charge at the same rate for his family). I also had Rachel join us in our sessions on three occasions and had them switch seats on my couch for part of it. I also had them play checkers together, which required Jared to touch pieces that she had touched. I also gave Jared ideas on how to be kind to Rachel, and while they did not become the best of friends, their relationship improved a great deal. During one session, Rachel began to cry and told Jared that she always looked up to him and loved having an older brother and how hurt she was by how Jared felt about her. To my amazement, Jared responded in a very mature and empathic way, and he apologized and explained that this was about OCD and not her. Jared did a great job and successfully completed his ladder. His parents were proud of him and they all complimented his determination in working through this. His mother and father were also relieved to not be burdened by OCD anymore. By the end of the 10-month long therapy, Jared no longer met the criteria for OCD, he and his sister got along much better, and the schedule at their parents' homes was in sync. In addition, he kept up with the meditation at night.

Case 4: Casey, Age 10, Fear of Doing Harm/ Overresponsibility Type

Description of Casey's OCD

Casey worried about doing something that could hurt someone, whether it was someone in her family, her friends, or strangers. She was constantly anticipating how her actions could impact someone else. For example, one day she was sneezing and got so worried that she was sick and would spread germs that would cause others to be sick, that she wore gloves and covered her mouth and nose with her turtleneck for days. She avoided touching anything that anyone else would touch. The gloves made it easier to do that, although her friends asked why she was wearing them. She had wanted to stay home from school, but her parents wouldn't let her (they had a rule about staying home from school: only if you had a fever or were vomiting). At school, she made an excuse and said her hands were cold. She took them off only when sitting at her desk and writing; she wore them throughout lunch and recess and when touching any shared surface. Her worry about hurting others went well beyond this, though, and sometimes she felt she was going a little crazy. She stepped on someone's pencil that fell on the floor, and she didn't want to give it back until she cleaned it, because she worried that her shoe had germs that got on the pencil. She took it to the bathroom to wash off, and while in the bathroom, she worried that other germs had gotten on it so she wrapped it in a paper towel and gave it back to her classmate, who clearly thought her behavior was strange. When walking out of a shop with her mother, she held the door open for everyone because she worried about closing it on someone. She was constantly picking up trash with paper towels and moving potential obstacles from sidewalks, as she feared someone would trip. One time when driving down their street after a storm, she asked her mom to get out of the car and move some branches on the road. Her mom said, "No, it's okay," and then Casey became hysterical; her mom turned back and got out of the car, and they moved the branches to the side. This type of behavior was constant, and at least once a day there was something she insisted on doing to prevent someone else from getting hurt. Casey's teacher called her mother to say that the recess aide reported to the teacher that Casey wasn't playing with others on the playground, but instead was "spotting" kids on the monkey bars in case they would fall. Casey also asked the recess aide to tell kids to come down from the climbing area because she said it wasn't safe. The aide also told the teacher that Casey spent one recess picking up branches from the blacktop. Her mom realized that Casey had OCD, like several other people in their family, and brought her to a psychiatrist for treatment. The psychiatrist prescribed an SSRI and referred her to me for therapy.

Treatment of Casey's OCD

Casey related to the three parts of anxiety and OCD cycle and nodded in agreement to her mom who was in the first session with her. In the first session, we discussed how she has the "overresponsibility" type of OCD and that it makes it very hard for her to feel at ease. We discussed how she sees herself as different from other kids and that she sees them as careless. I asked her to consider that that may be true, but it could also be that she is overly concerned about risk and harm, which makes her focus on certain things. We outlined her cycle:

1. Event: Cough.
2. Thought/Urge: What if I'm sick? I have to make sure I don't give it to anyone.
3. Feeling: Nervous.

4. Action/Ritual: Stay away from others, wear gloves, don't breathe on others, breathe into turtleneck.

1. Driving in car and see a branch in the road.
2. We need to move that branch because someone may get in an accident if it gets caught under their car.
3. Nervous, scared.
4. Have mom pull over and move the branch off the road.

Casey and I discussed that when you don't give into the anxiety and prevent the ritual, you have to learn how to tolerate the anxiety. We talked about the goal of being able to "sit with" the anxiety without acting on it. We also discussed how the OCD is making her notice things that most other people wouldn't notice and that her sense of responsibility gets triggered. Casey learned that she would have to become an observer of her anxious thoughts and not a participant who acts on them. Doing the practice of detached mindfulness was very helpful for her. We also did a lot of relaxation training to help her tolerate the anxiety.

We made self-talk cards, and most of her favorite ones were on tolerating the discomfort and staying with the anxiety until it went away. She carried them with her and made a second set for the car. I also talked with Casey's teacher and recess aide to guide them on what to say to Casey to help her fight the OCD, and they were great. The recess aide cued Casey to use her self-talk and directed her to play and have fun; she also assured Casey that she was on top of kids who were not using the equipment correctly and told Casey to trust her to be the one with the responsibility. This helped a great deal, as Casey felt the aide's confidence in these statements.

We went through Casey's thinking errors, including catastrophizing, all-or-nothing thinking, selective attention (she believed that kids were reckless and at risk of being hurt and scanned the environment to confirm her beliefs), and thought-event fusion (she believed that if she thought about it, it would likely happen). For the fusion thoughts, we talked about how she gives too much importance to her thoughts in general (overimportance of thoughts) and that just having the thought did not mean it would happen or would even be more likely to happen. There are many things that could be dangerous or risky that she didn't notice; I explained that this is how OCD works—it highlights certain things and overlooks others, and it is not logical. We practiced the "stamping it OCD" strategy, making a handout of many of her OCD thoughts and writing "OCD" in big red letters over each thought, so it could not be read.

Casey's loop and uncertainty training recordings were very effective for her, and she listened 10 minutes a day for 4 weeks, then noticed an improvement:

> What if I end up hurting someone or missing something that could keep them safe? There are so many bad things that could happen and people miss so much. What if I get someone sick, and what if I get bathroom germs on someone's things? It's up to me to do the right thing especially since so many people do not. I feel better when I'm watching out for other kids at recess, because it would be so terrible if something happened to one of them. Spotting them is more important than playing.
>
> It's always possible that I will end up hurting someone or missing something that could keep someone safe. There are so many bad things that could happen and people miss so much. It is always possible that I will get someone sick or that I'll get bathroom germs on them. It's possible that if I didn't spot kids at recess then one of them will get hurt and it will be my fault.

Interestingly, the loop tape helped Casey with the detached mindfulness, as she was able to listen to her thoughts and more accurately see them as OCD. It helped in making her an observer of her thoughts.

Casey and I made her ladder, again with the hardest items on the top.

(top)	Put branches on sidewalk and leave them there.
	Drive around branches on road without moving them.

See kids acting recklessly during recess and don't tell the aide.
Step on someone's pencil with your shoe, then give it to them.
No gloves at school.
Close door on someone walking behind you while walking out.
Go to school with sniffles.
Litter a biodegradable cup.
Take a library book to the bathroom with you and then give back to library.
Play on playground (no spotting or talking to aide).
(bottom) Do everything without gloves.

Casey relied on the principle she learned from ACT, which was to expect and then tolerate the anxiety that came from not doing her rituals. She did very well with it, and her school was very supportive. The first step of getting her to stop wearing gloves was not as easy as she had originally ranked, so we moved it to the middle, and she broke it down into smaller steps to start. Her teacher was very supportive and agreed to hold her gloves for her except for the planned time she would use them (e.g., when going to the bathroom) while she was building up to not using them at all. Casey's mother was also very supportive, and when they were driving around looking for branches, she said all the right things that were consistent with self-talk and tolerating the discomfort. Casey did very well in therapy and told me that although it was still hard at times, she knew that as long as she prevented doing the behavior, the thoughts would go away. After 6 months of therapy, we slowed down to once a month for another year until she was ready to stop.

Case 5: Nico, Age 13, Doubting/Indecisive Type

Description of Nico's OCD

Nico's OCD centered on doubts and indecisiveness. It got to the point where he couldn't answer questions in a direct way. He typically answered with "I guess," or "I'm not sure," or "I don't know," and this really drove his parents crazy. He would often feel embarrassed because it would take him a long time to make decisions, and even when he finally did, he never felt it was the right one. His parents got annoyed with him for taking so long, and sometimes they would just make the decision for him. Nico went back and forth and kept weighing the good and bad parts of each decision, and how that decision would change how things turn out. He envied his friends who made decisions with ease and wouldn't look back. He started to think that his friends must know themselves better than he did. He wished things naturally seemed clearer to him, and he didn't know why he struggled with decisions, big and small. He constantly felt uneasy about his decisions, and the back and forth of which choice was better continued even after he finally chose. When ordering food in a restaurant, he would narrow it down to a few options, then would pick (or his parents would pick for him) out of pressure from the waiter. Once the food came, he typically would look at what others got and felt he made the wrong choice. He couldn't decide on snacks and could take 45 minutes to pick his afterschool snack. Seeing his struggle, his father (who worked from home) started to pick out two snacks for him and put a sign on the pantry that said, "Do not look in here. Your only two options are on the counter." This helped Nico, but he also felt that there must be better snacks in the pantry. Although most of his doubting came to decisions, he also doubted other things, such as if he had "real friends" or if his friendships were "real friendships," and if he really deserved his good grades because "his teacher helped him" or the "assignment wasn't a good measure of my knowledge." He questioned what he liked and was starting to have a hard time feeling joy or happiness because he kept questioning his experiences and the authenticity of his relationships. He told his parents that he "couldn't take it anymore," and they brought him in for therapy.

When I diagnosed Nico with OCD and some resulting mild depression, he was relieved. A part of him thought this was just who he was, and that was very disconcerting to him. I explained that his critique of his friendships and questioning if they are "real friends" was also part of the OCD, the same for his feeling about not deserving his grades (the doubt was not limited to just his decision making). In therapy, we discussed that the task of adolescence is to form his identity, and how his OCD was interfering with this natural process for him. The OCD was making him unsure about his experiences and about himself and his worth in general. We discussed how sometimes when OCD is untreated, a person can have mild depression that is secondary to the OCD and will go away once the OCD is treated.

Treatment of Nico's OCD

Nico learned about the three parts of anxiety and the OCD cycle; here are two of his examples:

1. Event: Someone asks you if you like rap music.
2. Thought/Urge: I'm not sure. I think I do, but compared to real fans of rap, I probably don't like it in the way they do.
3. Feeling: Anxious, uneasy.
4. Action/Ritual: Answer in an ambiguous way and reply, "Some of it, sometimes, I'm not always sure."

1. Ordering in a sub shop with friends after school.
2. There are so many options. What if I get something that's not so good? I'm not sure what's good here.
3. A bit uneasy, feeling pressured.
4. Ask two friends what they are getting and ask the cashier which one is better; order the one she suggests (avoid making the decision yourself).

After making self-talk cards, we did detached mindfulness (the two OCD thoughts included in the mix of 10 thoughts were "What if I order the wrong thing? We might not come back to this place" and "Mr. James helped me with the paper. He gave me many guidelines and revisions, so the grade is not really mine. I didn't deserve an A." We also went through his all-or-nothing thinking and "should" statements.

The most helpful strategies for Nico, though, were his loop recording and uncertainty training recording (which he merged into one long recording and played daily for 5 weeks) and doing the attention training technique (part of metacognitive therapy). We added the attention training technique after a few months because Nico felt that he was still having a lot of random doubting thoughts and was having a hard time getting his focus off of them. I made the attention-training technique recording for him (11 minutes long), and he listened twice a day for a week and then once a day for 3 more weeks; he was very determined (due to how time-consuming this was, we began this after his 5 weeks of listening every day to the other recordings). He found the attention training technique to be very beneficial.

The following was one of Nico's loop recordings (he had about 10 of them, because he kept adding new ones when he struggled with decisions he made):

> What if my friends are not really my friends? It seems like other kids have real friends and I don't think my friendships are the same. I wonder if I was different if they would still like me, or if I didn't do the same things if they would still like me. It is always possible that my friendships aren't real. It is always possible that I don't actually have any real friends and never will. It's possible that my friends don't know the real me and that if they did, they wouldn't like me. It's possible that they wouldn't be my friend any more if I didn't have the same interests they had or if I acted differently. It's always possible that I'm not who I really think I am and if I figure it out, that I won't have any friends because they were only friends with someone they thought was someone different.

Nico and I developed the following ladder to help with his indecisiveness:

(top)	State your preferences that inconvenience others.
	State your preferences.
	Firmly list your interests.
	Ask for help from teacher and say something confident about your work product.
	Say things to affirm friendships.
	Pick snack in pantry in 2 minutes.
	Pick a snack (five options) in 2 minutes.
	Order something you don't really want in a restaurant and eat it.
	Make a decision and don't question it.
	Decide on what to eat (within 10, 5, 3, 2 minutes).
	Answer definitely "yes" and "no."
(bottom)	Move a book from one table to another, be asked if you moved it, and answer "Yes."

To practice in session, we looked at menus and I had Nico pick out what he would order and timed him (with no guidance, it took him about 15 minutes in total; with a gentle push, he was able to do it in 5 minutes). I also had his father bring snacks for him to choose from in my office, and he picked his choice in 2 minutes. We did a lot of preparation in the session when it came to saying things to affirm friendships, asking for help from his teacher, and stating his interests and preferences. We did role-plays and made recordings of examples of what he could say, and this was very useful.

Nico was successful in overcoming his OCD, although it took a little over a year of weekly therapy. His father did a lot of the lower item practices with him, which was excellent. I worked with his parents to stay calm and not be reactive; I gave them a list of things to say in response to his OCD behaviors. Also, during the course of his therapy, Nico began exercising and swimming, which helped with his confidence.

Case 6: Sean, Age 11, Symmetry/Just Feels Right Type

Description of Sean's OCD

Sean's dads (he had two fathers) called him a perfectionist for a long time before they understood it as OCD. Sean had to have everything perfectly organized in his room, and he worked to make everything even and straight. At school, he kept his belongings perfectly organized and said he felt better and was better able to focus when it was all organized the right way. He was sensitive to the environment around him as well, in terms of things being orderly and aligned. There were several times when they had to leave a place because it was not neat enough or there was too much disorganization; he would become so anxious and activated that it was easier for him and his parents to just leave. For example, Sean couldn't go over his aunt's house, because it felt "like chaos" to him, and if his parents made him, he would sit outside on her porch to get away from the inside of the house. When in bed at night, his parents fixed the blanket so that it would be even on each side of the bed. Otherwise, he refused to go to sleep. He could see that his parents were getting annoyed with him, especially when he insisted that they say things in a certain way. At bedtime, he had a routine of saying "Goodnight Dad, I love you," and Dad would have to say "Goodnight Sean. I love you and sweet dreams, my boy," and then he would follow the same pattern with his Papa. If either parent rushed through it or didn't sound like he meant it, Sean would make them do it again, starting with Dad each time (even if Dad did it right; they both had to do it right in order for it to count). When his parents tried to challenge him on this, he either became angry and agitated or would cry and stay up for hours. They would end up deciding that sleep was too important, so they just gave in. Sean had other patterns that he did, including how he ate his food (he would only eat certain foods made by Dad, and others only if they were made by Papa) and how he organized his backpack for school—everything had a place. Even the way he dressed was impacted by his need for matching and symmetry; if he had black jeans that were faded and not "as black" as his sneakers, he refused to wear them. Once, he received an asymmetrical zip jacket for a gift, and he gave it away to charity because he felt so uncomfortable just looking at it. He was also very superstitious about the way he walked in the house: He avoided the fourth step and eighth step on the stairs, he walked around the staircase from the back before going up it, he avoided walking by a room just once, and would go back and rewalk in front of it, which gave him a sense of safety for that room. He worried about bad things happening if his fathers didn't say "I love you" each time they said goodbye to him or each other. His parents were exhausted, and it seemed to be getting worse, so they brought him in for therapy.

In therapy, we talked about perfectionism, when perfectionism occurs as part of OCD, and how he met the criteria for diagnosis. We discussed the power of OCD in impacting his everyday experience and causing stress for everyone in the home. His behavior didn't accurately reflect the close, secure attachment he had with his parents.

Treatment of Sean's OCD

We reviewed the three parts of anxiety and the OCD cycle and went through several examples. We discussed perfectionism and the "just feels right" type of OCD. The focus on his therapy would be on adapting to the different environments and conditions that did not "feel right" for him, rather than avoiding or changing them. A large part of this would be learning how to tolerate discomfort and things not feeling, or seeming, right.

I went through calm breathing, one-nostril breathing, progressive muscle relaxation, and several apps with Sean. Of these, he liked the calm breathing and apps the most; in particular, he liked the "CBT Tools for Youth" app and listened to the "Awareness meditation" on it several times a day in the beginning. We made many self-talk cards, especially those on tolerating the discomfort and staying with the anxiety until it dissolved. He also liked the ones I made on facing his fears, being proactive, and not giving into the OCD. We went through his thinking errors, which were mostly magical thinking, superstitious thinking, and all-or-nothing thinking. We made handouts on being proactive versus reactive. We did not make a loop recording or do detached mindfulness; rather, we focused all of our energy on working on his ladder, included below, which took a lot of energy for him every day.

(top)	Eliminate bedtime goodnight routine (parents go to bed without saying goodnight).
	Sleep over at aunt's house.
	Vary bedtime goodnight routine (tone; how it is said).
	Vary bedtime goodnight routine (what is said).
	Vary bedtime goodnight routine (rush through it).
	Vary bedtime goodnight routine (different order).
	Go to aunt's house for 30 minutes, 1 hour, 3 hours.
	Dad leaves without saying "Goodbye."
	Papa leaves without saying "Goodbye."
	Dad leaves without saying "I love you."
	Papa leaves without saying "I love you."
	Walk on eighth step.
	Walk on fourth step.
	Wear asymmetrical hoodie.
	Walk on staircase from the front.
	Walk by a room just once.
	Wear different shades of black.
	Eat pancakes made by Dad.
	Eat eggs made by Papa.

Eat chicken made by Dad.
Go to antique shop that is cluttered and messy.
Keep belongings out of place at school.
Put four to five things out of place in room and leave them for 5 days.
Be in living room when things are out of place.
Move two things out of place in your room and leave them that way for 2 days.
(bottom) Leave part of your backpack unorganized.

Sean's parents were an integral part of his success. They met with me several times to review how they could change their response to his triggers and what to say and do to support him when facing his fears. His parents prompted him to do the practices, and they often modeled it for him before he practiced (e.g., Dad made his own work bag unorganized, and they moved things out of place in their own room as well). Sean's treatment was a huge success, and he navigated his ladder quite well. He repeated most of the steps several times before moving onto the next one. Sean graduated from therapy after 8 months, then saw me a few more times for follow-up sessions.

Case 7: Ashley, Age 12, Need to Confess Type

Description of Ashley's OCD

Being picked up from school was a relief for Ashley—she would tell her mom every detail of the day that she felt unsure about. Her mom would listen, and at first, Ashley wanted her mom to tell her everything she did was okay, but then she was satisfied with her mom just listening and saying nothing afterward. Ashley felt it was enough as long as her mom heard everything she was concerned about, because she knew if she did anything wrong or if anything she said was bad or alarming, that her mom would have a reaction that would indicate disapproval. As long as there was no reaction, she was safe.

Once in the car, she would "confess" all of the things she worried about. For example, she would say,

> When I got to school I was rushing in and I think the door behind me might not have closed all the way and it's supposed to be locked for safety. I'm not sure, because I was walking so fast, but I think I heard the door shutting but I think someone could have snuck in behind me and I'm not sure who it was because I didn't look back and I'm worried it might not be a student but might be someone who is trying to hurt a student and then I would've let that happen, but I'd probably know by now if something happened. Tomorrow I'm going to be sure that I close the door completely once I walk in. Then I stepped on a pencil but I'm not sure if it was a pencil but it felt like one and I don't know maybe it was something else. I went to the bathroom and as I was pulling out some toilet paper I think some of it at the end touched the floor which is gross but I still used it and maybe I got germs in me which would be really bad. At lunch there was this girl who looked like she wanted to sit with us but no one made room and most of the girls didn't even notice her, but I did and I didn't say anything but she didn't either and then just walked away. I'm not sure that I'm such a nice person and why wouldn't I have just scooted over and invited her to sit with us? Also I was raising my hand to answer a question in math but I put my hand up after the boy in front of me put his hand up and the teacher called on me and I got the answer right and I should've let him be called on because he put his hand up first. I was also rushing a few times out of class and forgot to say goodbye to two of my teachers which is so mean.

Ashley's mom would listen and pause a few moments after Ashley finished, then she would talk about their dinner plans. She didn't asked Ashley anything about school because when she did, it would trigger even more confessions. Once at home, Ashley would report to Mom things she noticed outside or in the house that she felt may be a concern, and when Mom would tell her she didn't need to report anything, Ashley would say she worried that if she didn't tell her mom and something bad happened, that she would be responsible and to blame. Her mother realized that Ashley's need to confess was chipping away at their relationship, and she felt most of what they spoke about centered on the confessions. She took Ashley to the pediatrician and asked for some blood work to see if there was something imbalanced making her act this way. The pediatrician diagnosed her with OCD and referred her to me.

Treatment of Ashley's OCD

Ashley had never heard of OCD before, so I explained the disorder and anxiety in general. We discussed her obsessions and compulsions and how the OCD caused her to second guess everything she did. The OCD was taking up so much of her time and energy and also interfered with her normal relationship with her mom.

I taught her calm breathing and relaxation, and several yoga moves, which she enjoyed. We made self-talk cards and went through the thinking errors (catastrophizing, shoulds, all-or-nothing, selective attention). We talked about the themes of "overimportance of thoughts," "overresponsibility," "desire for certainty," and "overestimation of danger," and she related to all of them. She even commented, "That describes how it is for me every day!" We did detached mindfulness and rotated four OCD thoughts in the two spots of the 10-thought rotation, including: "What's wrong with me that I would put my school in jeopardy like that?", "I should've let the teacher call on Brad and not raise my hand first," "Why didn't I invite that girl to sit with us—what's wrong with me!", and "I stepped on someone's pencil and contaminated it." The detached mindfulness and "stamping it

OCD" approach was very helpful in getting Ashley to know her OCD thoughts and correctly identify them as OCD.

Ashley made a few loop recordings; I limited her to only two as I did not want them to become a form of confessing, but wanted to be able to give her some insight into how she sounded. One of her recordings came from the following script:

> Once I tell Mom, I'll feel better. When I got to school I was rushing and I'm not sure if I closed the door all the way and I think someone came in behind me but I never looked—I don't know why I didn't turn around, so stupid—and now I'm thinking I let a bad man into the building and maybe he is still there I don't know. I better be more careful and starting tomorrow I am going to make sure it's closed all the way and may even stay until right before the bell. I also stepped on something and I'm not sure what it was, maybe a pencil, and I might have broken it, and also when I was in the bathroom I think the end of the toilet paper touched the floor and then I used it which was dumb and now I might have contaminated myself. Also there was this girl at lunch and I'm pretty sure she wanted to sit with us but I didn't do anything and then she walked away. I don't think anyone other than me even saw her and I don't know why I didn't just make room for her, it would have been so easy. I also raised my hand after Brad's hand went up but the teacher called on me and that was just wrong of me, period.
>
> I saw this man walking in front of our house on the street and I usually don't see anyone and then this car drove by slowly, I think they were looking at our house. I also noticed that one of the boxes on the side of our house was somewhat open and maybe someone was trying to cut the cords inside. There are so many crazy and bad things that can happen and I have to tell Mom so she makes sure it's okay and that nothing bad happens. I can't have something bad happen because I decided not to say anything. It's always better to say something.

The loops were helpful in giving her perspective, but it was the ladder that helped Ashley overcome OCD. Included below is the ladder we constructed based on her symptoms.

(top)	Leave front door to school slightly open after walking in.
	Walk through front door of school and don't check that it was closed.
	Rush while walking in and don't look behind you.
	Intentionally exclude someone from a conversation.
	Notice something that could be a hazard or risk and don't report it.
	Step on someone's pencil with your shoe, then give it to them.
	Leave class without saying goodbye to teachers.
	Listen to music, no talking.
	Mom talks for 5 minutes.
	Listen to book on tape.
	Play recording of normal dialogue (no confessions).
	Get in car and limit confessing (5 minutes, 3 minutes, 1 minute).
	Play recording of previous confessions.
	Before getting in car, make recording of confessions and don't play.
(bottom)	Before getting in car, make recording of confessions and play for Mom.

One of the most helpful first steps is to delay or switch up a ritual. This does a great job challenging the ritual, and the child is usually willing to vary it in some way, especially when compared to the option of eliminating it completely. By delaying or varying a ritual, it loses some of its power and also becomes easier to eventually stop doing it. Ashley's mom was an integral part of the treatment process, as she was the one who had to give the cue to disrupt or limit the confessing. She was highly motivated and ended up being the perfect combination of firm and supportive. We discussed how if Ashley wouldn't stop the confessing, that Mom could blare music or pull over and get of the car to dramatically challenge the OCD (and she ended up doing both several times, all of which was extremely effective, particularly as this was uncharacteristic behavior on the part of her mom, which made it clear to Ashley that she was engaging in OCD).

Ashley's therapy lasted about 5 months. Her mom did a great job with ensuring that she didn't give into the rituals, and that made it shorter. About 6 months after she graduated from therapy, Ashley's symptoms returned in a milder version. Her mother and I considered that it was due to hormonal changes, given that she had started menstruation. She came in for six additional sessions, and we resumed having her listen to the loop recording and made a mini-ladder; she did great and quickly returned to being symptom-free. Due to her relapse, we decided to do check-in appointments every 3–4 months for another year. At these appointments, we would go through her folder with all of the strategies and review what she should do in case it comes back.

Case 8: Chris, Age 14, Scrupulosity Type

Description of Chris's OCD

Chris has the scrupulosity type of OCD. Prior to treatment, he understood his symptoms as evidence that he was a bad person and would be punished by God. He had what he labeled as "impure" thoughts, and no matter what he did to get rid of them, they kept coming up. He felt that there must be something wrong with him or that he must be a pervert or weird. Last year, a girl told him that she liked him, but he avoided her, and she eventually lost interest. He was not comfortable dating because he didn't trust his thoughts and what they said about him, and she was such a nice girl that he didn't want her to date someone who could be a pervert. When Chris shared his "impure" thoughts with me, it turned out that they were just normal thoughts for someone his age. He pictured himself kissing different girls and worried that it meant he was going to kiss them against their will. He also felt incredibly guilty if he judged someone or when he was annoyed with his friends. He concluded that if he had these negative thoughts about his friends, then he didn't deserve them. Chris had a lot of "shoulds" that he used to categorize his thoughts, such as "I shouldn't say bad things about others," "I should always see the best in others," and "Good people should always offer to help." If a bad or impure thought came up, he would do something "good" to help balance it out. For example, he would offer to help out at home, do a chore without being asked, clean his room, or study. He felt these good things compensated for his bad thoughts. This feeling of being bad or doing something wrong had been getting worse, and his father asked him why he was always offering to help. His father told him that he should be more rebellious like his father was at his age. Chris opened up to his dad and told him that he didn't think he was a good person, and being rebellious would confirm it. After that, his father got a referral for therapy for Chris.

Treatment of Chris's OCD

Like Nico, Chris's OCD was interfering with his identity development and the normal process of developing romantic feelings that typically defines the adolescent period. Chris and I discussed how his OCD was attacking his concept of "who he is" and that this is how OCD was making him vulnerable and gained power over him. Because Chris was religious, we ended up having him meet with his pastor, who gave him assurance that he was a good person, and told him that he was made in God's image so he couldn't inherently be impure or bad. The pastor also normalized for Chris that boys his age are allowed to like girls of a similar age and added that he could trust that Chris was a respectful and kind person at the core. He also told Chris that if he had a daughter, he would be relieved if she liked someone as kind and sensitive as Chris. This was very helpful for him to hear; although an accommodation to his OCD in a way (reassurance), it provided a foundation for us toward the beginning of his treatment to be able to make progress on discrediting these thoughts. Basically, the pastor helped Chris see these thoughts as symptoms of OCD and also validated that Chris was a good person.

I explained the three parts of anxiety and the OCD cycle and taught him relaxation. We discussed how meditation would be particularly useful for him, and he regularly used the Insight Timer app. We went through the OCD themes, such as "overimportance of thoughts" and "rigid/moral thinking." I explained that these thoughts were experienced by him as "wrong" and helped him to differentiate from a bad person by explaining that a bad person wouldn't ever think about any (even imagined) violation of a girl (kissing her against her will) as wrong—a bad person would instead justify it to himself. So, essentially he couldn't be bad because he was so worried about and afraid of hurting a girl. Chris also learned the difference between thinking or imagining something sexual (normal) and acting on it. We also discussed how kissing a girl is normal for a 14-year-old, and as long as it is mutual, it is healthy. I explained that sexual development is a process; you don't just suddenly become an adult who has sex, rather you start out by liking someone, talking to her, holding hands, kissing, and that it is gradual and progressive. We discussed how he was judging himself for having normal thoughts about friends; I explained that sometimes friends annoy us and sometimes friends are rude, and there is nothing wrong with noticing and thinking these thoughts. Even if he got annoyed and acted annoyed with a friend, this would still be within the range of what is appropriate and normal in a close friendship.

I made many self-talk cards for Chris, and he took photos of them and kept them on his phone. One that was particularly useful for him was: "OCD is not an accurate predictor of who I am. OCD wants me to question myself, but I don't have to listen to it. I know who I am and what I'm worth. Even if I'm not always perfect, I am fundamentally a good person." We also made an uncertainty training recording using this script:

It is always possible that I'm a bad person and want to hurt others. It's always possible that my impure thoughts are my real thoughts and truly reflect who I am. It's possible that I really am a pervert or a weirdo. It's always possible that if I dated that girl, I would have hurt her and forced myself on her. It's possible that I couldn't trust myself. I might be a bad person. I say bad things about my friends in my head. It's always possible that I'm not a real friend.

We made the following ladder:

(top)	Share feelings with a girl.
	Have social plan with a girl.
	Text a girl.
	Talk to a girl.
	Purposely have judging thought about a friend, then ask that friend for a favor.
	Make list of flaws in friends and others.
	Purposely do something rude without apologizing.
	Refuse to do chore parents ask you to do.
	Have impure thought and don't clean.
(bottom)	Have impure thought and write it down.

It is noteworthy that some of these ladder items reflect poor values or may not be examples of good social thinking; however, these steps are necessary to go against the OCD. Again, research shows that the more extreme exposures are more helpful. In addition, practicing these behaviors would not cause Chris's values to change.

Chris did a great job in therapy; he came every week for a year before slowing down to once every 3 weeks for another few months. The practices on the ladder were instrumental in his progress. He needed to have the behavioral exposures, especially those involving girls, to overcome his OCD. He ended up dating the girl who initially liked him. She was confident and expressive, and he grew comfortable taking the initiative to hold her hand and be close to her. From a therapy perspective, she was the ideal first girl for him to like because she made her feelings known, with no ambiguity. Chris's case is another example of why treatment is so important in terms of preventing a disruption in psychological development. His identity formation could've been seriously damaged if his OCD wasn't treated. Because OCD thinking can be so strong, scary, and loud, it can often be hard to fight back. Chris's treatment was comprehensive, and we worked to make sure he was confident about who he was as a person, separate from any OCD.

Case 9: Ana, Age 12, Scrupulosity Type

Description of Ana's OCD

Ana also had the scrupulosity type, but her dilemma centered on sexual themes. She never thought much about gender, but when her friend told her that she was unsure if she was really a girl, Ana started to wonder about her own gender as well. She then started to worry that she might be a lesbian, even though she didn't have sexual feelings (toward either gender) yet. She also felt guilty about her worries about being a lesbian, because she knew that there was nothing wrong with being a lesbian, but she was bothered by the idea of it. Then she thought that this is probably what people who are lesbians think when they first realize that they are lesbians. When she was in P.E. and changing for class, if she looked over at one of her friends and saw her friend without a shirt, she thought she must have looked over on purpose because she wanted to see her friend naked. She tried to rush and be quick when changing. At a sleepover party, she and all of her friends were sleeping in sleeping bags on the floor, and she had the thought, *What if I touch my friend while I'm sleeping?*, as if her unconscious would make her do something she didn't want to do consciously. She avoided the next sleepover, leaving before the sleeping part. Having these thoughts led to more thoughts, including ones about being a pedophile; Ana started to think she couldn't trust herself and worried that she would harm other children. She worried that she might molest them. Ana got very upset about these thoughts and wondered where they came from. She had never had any inappropriate thoughts like this, and then, suddenly, they were happening regularly. When her little cousins came over and climbed on her bed, she got particularly anxious; she asked her brother to come in her room, too, because she knew nothing would happen if he was there. She also sat on her hands when they were in her room to ensure that she wouldn't touch them. Ana was repulsed and embarrassed by these thoughts and knew it was not normal to think this way; she thought, *Something must be wrong with me.* She was an exceptional student and very social, but all of these thoughts were distracting her, and her grades began to slip. She also had stomachaches on most days. Finally, she spoke with the school counselor about the thoughts she was having about being a lesbian. The school counselor asked for permission to talk with her parents, and she made a referral for therapy for Ana's OCD.

Treatment of Ana's OCD

Ana was very uncomfortable talking about her thoughts, so I told her that her parents shared the theme of her thoughts with me, and we didn't need to discuss them specifically just yet. This made the initial appointment more tolerable for her. I explained that she met the criteria for OCD and that she had the scrupulosity type, which commonly involved sexual themes. She felt a great deal of shame and confusion about her thoughts. She truly felt that there must be something "really wrong" with her. I explained that these feelings are all normal for OCD. We discussed obsessions as "unwanted, intrusive thoughts" and talked about how this is very different from the typical process someone goes through when coming out as lesbian or questioning one's gender identity. In order to be able to challenge the OCD, I had to challenge the validity of her thoughts about being a pedophile. We also talked about how pedophiles typically do not consider themselves to be pedophiles, and do not feel guilty or remorseful, but rather justified in their behavior (they also don't try to come to therapy to work on their thoughts). I told her that I will often have clients who come to me with worries that they are "going crazy," and I explain that people with psychosis don't ever think they are "going crazy" or that they are "crazy"; rather, they think you are crazy if you challenge their delusions or hallucinations. Similarly, pedophiles don't worry that they are pedophiles. Ana benefitted from my confidence about her diagnosis. I normalized her coming to me by explaining that I only see people with anxiety disorders and OCD, so if she is coming to me, it's because she has anxiety or OCD, not because she is a pedophile! I explained that what was "wrong" with her was that she has OCD, nothing more and nothing less, and assured her that OCD is a treatable condition and that there is a plan to follow to overcome it. I also told her that her experience didn't seem to reflect what I typically saw in the coming out process for lesbians, but that if she was lesbian we'd only really be able to know this once the OCD was treated. Ana told her parents that she felt relieved by coming to the appointment!

We reviewed the three parts of anxiety and OCD cycle. Here is an example of hers:

1. Event: Talking to friend while changing for P.E.
2. Thought/Urge: I think I'm looking at her chest. Why am I looking at her? I think this means I'm a lesbian.
3. Feeling: Anxious, shameful.
4. Action/Ritual: Look away, speed up the changing, don't talk to anyone next time in locker room.

Ana and I made self-talk cards and went through her thinking errors. I explained thought-action fusion, which was her main thinking error: She worried that by having the thought that she was going to inappropriately touch her cousins or friends while sleeping over, then it meant she was going to do it. We also did detached mindfulness, which was helpful. We discussed her themes of "desire for certainty," "overimportance of thoughts," and "rigid/moral thinking."

She made a loop recording using the following script:

What if I'm a lesbian? What if I'm really a boy? What if these thoughts mean I am a lesbian or that I have gender confusion? Why else would I be having these thoughts? And I must be biased because there is nothing wrong with being a lesbian or wanting to be a different gender. What if I'm really a lesbian but I don't know it? At P.E. I think I'm checking my friend's body out. What if I act on these feelings at a sleepover and what if I touch my friend's privates? That might be rape! What if I did that when I was sleeping and didn't know it because it was my urge that I never knew about? What if I molest my cousins? Oh my God, that would be terrible. The whole family would freak out. Why would I even think that way? There must be something wrong with me. Normal people don't think this way!

It is always possible that I am a lesbian. It's always possible that I am really a boy. It's possible that having these thoughts means I am a lesbian or have gender confusion. It's possible that the only reason I would be having these thoughts is because I am a lesbian or really am a boy. It's possible that I am a homophobe. It's always possible that I'm really a lesbian and don't know it. It's possible that I am checking my friend's body out because I am lesbian. It's always possible that I will act on these feelings at a sleepover and will touch my friend's privates. It's possible that that would be rape, and it's possible that I would do it when I was sleeping and wouldn't even know I was doing it. It's possible that I will molest my cousin and that my family would disown me. It's always possible that I am a pedophile because I am thinking like one.

Ana's loop recording was a huge trigger for her. She also worried that making it meant that there was evidence on her phone that she was a pedophile. I reiterated that we were making a loop recording because she has OCD and that listening to it at first was going to trigger her and cause her anxiety to rise, but that with repetition, it would go down. I reiterated that it's the thought, not the content of the thought (what the thought is about), that she's desensitizing to. Every one has different content, but OCD thoughts are just OCD thoughts. We listened to the loop together for 25 minutes each session, and I had her come in twice a week for the first month. By the second week, she was able to listen alone, and it was very useful. She completely desensitized to these thoughts, and they eventually stopped coming up. She was still uncomfortable with some of the situations, but she wasn't having the bothersome thoughts anymore.

Ana also made the following ladder.

(top)	Be around cousins alone (no sitting on hands).
	Invite cousins to play on your bed (play cards).
	Go to a sleepover and stay the whole time—sleep in sleeping bags.
	Talk to a friend while changing in P.E. and look in her direction.
	Read article about girl considering her gender identity.
	Read article about girl coming out as lesbian.
(bottom)	Take a long time to change in P.E.

We reviewed the three keys principles to doing her ladder—repetition, frequency, and staying in the situation for a prolonged period of time (for habituation to occur)—and she used these principles in her practice. The E/RP was very useful. The loop recording combined with the ladder was transformative for Ana. After 9 months of coming to therapy on a regular basis, we slowed down to once or twice a month, and after 4 more months, she was diagnosis-free and graduated from therapy.

Case 10: Kaitlyn, Age 8, "Bad" Thoughts Type

Description of Kaitlyn's OCD

Kaitlyn had always been a sensitive and intense child. Even as a toddler, her parents described how they had a sense that she was anxious and fearful, as she required a great deal of soothing and attention in order to calm down when she got upset and also when going to sleep at night. In first grade, she started asking questions related to safety, such as "Are there bad people in the world? What if they come in our house? How will you keep me safe? What if someone's hiding in a closet?" Bedtime was a constant struggle, and starting in second grade after she had trouble adjusting to a new teacher, she started washing her hands for lengthy periods. She would be in the bathroom more often and for longer times. Her parents also noticed that she was touching the tips of her fingers together in a certain pattern and moving her shoulders back and forth, seemingly on purpose. She explained, "I feel better when I wash my hands. It helps get rid of the bad thoughts." Never telling her parents the content of these "bad thoughts," it was obvious that they caused her a great deal of distress. The handwashing became more and more frequent, and her hands appeared red with cracked skin that would often bleed. She also touched her fingers together in the pattern and moved her shoulders back and forth at least 10 times a day. She seemed tired and irritable much of the time and had a hard time recovering from minor setbacks. Her teacher was getting annoyed with how often she asked to use the bathroom during the day; she also felt Kaitlyn wasn't paying good attention. Her parents spoke with her pediatrician about these symptoms, and the pediatrician referred Kaitlyn for therapy.

In therapy, Kaitlyn learned that these "bad thoughts" that kept popping up were called "obsessions" and that the handwashing and finger touching and shoulder adjusting were "compulsions" that she did in response to the anxiety she felt from the obsessions. I explained that she didn't do anything wrong, that these thoughts were not her fault, and expressed how sorry I was that she had felt so scared for such a long time. She learned that, because of the time it was taking (more than 1 hour a day) and the interference it was causing in her life (trouble sleeping, missing class time, trouble paying attention, irritability), that she met the criteria for OCD. Kaitlyn immediately felt better; the fact that there was a name for it gave her an explanation for what was happening to her for all this time. We worked together to address her concerns and discomfort with sharing the actual thoughts, and I told her that by sharing them, she would take some of OCD's power away; by keeping the thoughts to herself, she not only missed the benefit of externalizing them, but she also gave the thoughts more power. I explained that it would feel scary at first to share the thoughts and offered for her to write them down instead; however, she was more afraid to write them as she felt it would make the thoughts more true. I offered to have her type them on a computer that we could delete as soon as she wrote them. She ended up sharing the thoughts verbally, but giving her the options to describe the thoughts in different ways made her more likely to share them (e.g., it became more like "Which way will you choose?" as opposed to "Are you ready to tell me the thoughts?").

Ultimately, revealing what the thoughts were was a turning point for her, as she had never heard herself *say* the thoughts, and when she did, they became externalized and she realized that they were quite extreme; it was like a reality check in a way. Her thoughts were accompanied by images, which were what made her feel so scared. The thoughts were bad, but the images were worse. Mostly, the bad thoughts came during the first hour of being in school and again at bedtime; she still had the thoughts at other times but was able to wash her hands and move onto something else, whereas it was harder to do that when at school and nearly impossible to do at bedtime. The thoughts centered on her parents, sister, or herself being harmed; she worried about break-ins and that they would all be killed. The thoughts varied in terms of who was killed—sometimes it was her mother or her father, sometimes it was both, sometimes it was her mother, father, and sister, and she was left alone, and sometimes it was all four of them. She imagined a bloody scene and being unable to escape, and reported that she often had trouble breathing or would breathe fast while having these thoughts. Although she had little exposure to scary movies or news images, she had heard a few scary stories that kids in her neighborhood had shared (keep in mind that most children without OCD or the predisposition for it would have forgotten these stories a day or two after hearing them). OCD ran in her family: Her paternal grandmother and paternal uncle had it, as did one of her cousins. Although neither of her parents had OCD, they both had the tendency to get anxious, particularly her father who described himself as a "chronic worrier, always looking for what could go wrong."

In terms of accommodations, before bedtime, she called out to say goodnight to her sister and make sure she was in her room. She also checked the front and back door locks. Kaitlyn had her parents leave her closet light on with the door wide open. Some nights, she asked her parents to check their closets and leave the hallway light on. They had a home security system, and before bed, Kaitlyn would remind her parents, "Don't forget to put the alarm on." Her parents reminded her that she was safe and that nothing bad would happen to her. They stayed with her at night until she feel asleep, which would sometimes take an hour or longer. Most nights, she would wake up in the middle of the night and come into their room and sleep in their bed. They were exhausted, yet they felt terrible for her as they saw how fearful she had become. Her sister, who was 3 years older, felt annoyed that she had hardly any time with their parents at bedtime and expressed that she would like to be able to read in bed with her mother reading next to her, and told her parents that it is "unfair and annoying that no one can read next to me." Although she was kind to Kaitlyn, she resented how much time Kaitlyn took from their parents. Usually, by the time a family comes in for therapy, they are depleted and at their wit's end. It takes a few months before progress is made, yet most families begin to feel more hope and energized by taking action and getting their child into treatment.

Treatment of Kaitlyn's OCD

I started with an explanation of the three parts of anxiety and the OCD cycle. We went through her cycle, and because the thoughts just popped up without a clear or specific trigger, the thought itself was the activating event:

1. Have bad thought or image.
2. Think and believe that the bad thought means something bad will happen (that the thought will become real).
3. Anxious and scared.
4. Wash hands several times and do finger touching pattern to neutralize the thought.

Seeing the cycle helped Kaitlyn to better understand her experience and see it as OCD. We worked on calm breathing also. She liked one-nostril breathing, which we planned on her using at bedtime before getting into bed and again once in bed. I also introduced her to the Calm app, which she really liked (particularly the "Sleep Stories," which helped her relax before bed). We discussed her practicing lying in bed during the daytime, using the app to help reassociate her bed with relaxation. I taught her progressive muscle relaxation and gave her a few Yoga Pretzel cards so she could practice three yoga poses to help her unwind before bed and get more "in her body."

I made Kaitlyn many self-talk cards, and she picked her four favorites to memorize, including: "Thoughts are just thoughts. Thoughts have no power unless I give them power," "I'm scared, but I'm safe," "In this moment, I am fine. Everything is okay," and "This is just the OCD talking." We did detached mindfulness, and the two OCD thoughts we included were: (1) "What if someone breaks in and hurts us?" and (2) "What if we all get killed?" Seeing these thoughts mixed in with other neutral thoughts helped Kaitlyn understand that the OCD thoughts were just thoughts and nothing else.

She also recorded a loop and uncertainty training recording from this typed script:

What if there are bad people out there who come and try to hurt us? What if someone breaks in? What if we don't hear them coming in? What if there is someone hiding in the closet? What if the images come true and we are all killed? What if they kill my parents? What if they kill my sister? What if my parents and my sister die and I am left alone? What if they kill me, and then my parents will be so sad? What if we all get killed? What if there will be a lot of blood? What if I am unable to escape? What if we are all trapped? What if we forget to put the alarm on and they come in? What if my sister is downstairs and they get her and we don't know she was taken?

It is always possible that there are bad people out there who will come and hurt us. It is always possible someone will break in. It is always possible that we won't hear the bad people who are breaking in. It is always possible that someone is hiding in the closet. It's possible that what I imagine will come true and we will all be killed. It is always possible that they will kill my parents or kill my sister or that both of them will die and I will be left alone. It's always possible that they will kill me, and my parents will be so sad. It's always possible that we will all get killed. It's always possible that there will be a lot of blood. It's possible we won't be able to escape and that we will be trapped. It's always possible we will forget to put the alarm on and they will come in. It's possible my sister will be downstairs and they will get her and we won't even know she was taken.

Kaitlyn listened to this recording, which was almost 2 minutes in length, seven times in a row (14 minutes) every day for a week, then five times in a row (10 minutes) for 2 more weeks. By the third week, she said the thoughts no longer sounded like real thoughts to her and she was able to listen without getting triggered. In addition, the thoughts were occurring less often, and she was more able to switch away from them.

Kaitlyn and I made a ladder with her fears, and we used this to do the Exposure/Response Prevention (the harder items on the top, the easier items on the bottom).

(top)	Only Dad puts you to bed while Mom reads with sister.
	Go to bed on own without checking doors.

Go to bed on own without saying goodnight to sister.
Go to bed on own.
Go to bed on own (Mom stays with you for 30, 20, 10 minutes).
Go to bed without checking doors.
Go to bed without saying goodnight to sister.
Go to bed without checking on sister (can still say goodnight).
Closet door closed, lights off.
Closet door closed, lights on.
Stay in bed throughout the night.
Have a bad thought—no washing.
Have a bad thought—delay washing.
Have a bad thought—no finger/shoulder.
Have a bad thought—delay finger/shoulder.
Go to bed without reminding parents to put alarm on.
Go to bed without asking parents if they have locked door.

(bottom)

We decided to leave the hallway light on, as it seemed to be more of a preference for her, and this one potential accommodation did not cause a disruption to anyone in the house and did not prevent her from falling or staying asleep. A big part of the treatment was training Kaitlyn's parents on how to respond to her differently; they learned how to answer her questions in a way that supported her to use her strategies to fight the OCD. They learned how to answer without providing reassurance and even on occasion would say, "I wish I could reassure you, but that would be making the OCD worse, and I can't do that." They stopped telling her that nothing bad will happen and became supportive of the exposure work by saying, "We can't know for sure; trying to know for sure makes the OCD happy, and we want the OCD to go away."

Kaitlyn navigated her way through the ladder in a linear, well-paced way. She was motivated to complete it, and her parents were aware of what she was working on each day and were very supportive and encouraging. Once she faced her fears and stopped all the checking and avoidance behavior, she felt stronger. She worked very hard in therapy, especially when it came to the images. Kaitlyn learned how to tolerate the distress and found that when she did that, the image would go away faster. She would say out loud, "It's only OCD," or "If I didn't have OCD, I wouldn't have images, so the images are not real." She fought the OCD and won. After 8 months of weekly therapy, we slowed down to twice a month, and then a few months after that, she graduated. At our last celebration session, I complimented her commitment to therapy and noted that she worked very hard the whole time. As with all of my clients, I reminded Kaitlyn that she could come back in the future if needed.

Summary

It is my goal that from reviewing these detailed case examples that you will have a comprehensive picture of what OCD symptoms and OCD treatment look like. The more informed you are as your child's parent, the more prepared you will be to ensure that your child is receiving top-notch and thorough treatment. In the case of OCD and other anxiety disorders, being well-versed in what CBT treatment entails gives you a significant advantage that will benefit your child tremendously.

These examples include the most common cases of OCD and some less common cases; however, there are other presentations of OCD and many other OCD symptoms that are not expressed here. Each child or teen with OCD will have her own specific rituals that are unique to her; the goal is to figure them out and help the child understand that they are just symptoms of OCD. Many children, especially teenagers, are worried that they have more than OCD. For example, teens who have the scrupulosity type focused on sexual themes worry that their symptoms indicate that they are a true sexual deviant and are perverted. They may ask, "Why would I have these thoughts if I wasn't a pervert (or pedophile)?" and it is essential that you answer with confidence and assure them that it is "only OCD." Similarly, children and teens with OCD may have a fear of going crazy. They are so stuck in their thoughts that it can be hard to see themselves outside of the OCD. They are thinking the same thoughts over and over, they are thinking about their thoughts and anxious about the thought itself (content), and they are thinking the fact that they are having all of these thoughts. All of this naturally makes them feel that they are going crazy. It is important to clarify that OCD makes people feel this way, but that is not what's happening. They are not going crazy and won't lose their minds. These reassurances are necessary in the beginning, and then the child will ultimately desensitize to these thoughts during the treatment (e.g., from the loop recordings).

It is often the case that OCD is either accompanied by another anxiety disorder or depression, and these problems need to be treated as well. Usually, if the depression is secondary to the OCD, it will naturally improve when the OCD is treated; however, you may need to encourage or work with the child to resume normal activities, including social ones. Depression can causes the child to isolate, and even when the depression is gone, she may be in a rut and require some behavioral activation to get her to return to all activities. In resuming all activities, the depression lifts even further.

Perfectionism may or may not be a symptom of OCD. Many times, I will treat a child with OCD, and we do perfectionism work as well. Children with perfectionism can often engage in "people-pleasing," and when this happens I work with them on being more assertive and expressing their preferences. For teens, I have them read *The Disease to Please* by Harriet B. Braiker.

I collaborate as much as possible with other providers (psychiatrists, pediatricians, other doctors) and the school teachers and certain staff. For example, in the case of food allergies and OCD, I collaborated with an allergist who gave me guidelines and endorsed the exposures I had proposed.

Case Examples: Bringing It All Together

The cases described in this chapter are all treatment successes. Although the goal and standard should be to eliminate the OCD, again, there are cases where the OCD is improved but not gone. It can become a management issue, but it is important to try treatment again in the future.

Chapter 8

What to Expect on the Road Ahead

OCD may or may not be a long-lasting disorder. The goal is to treat it by resolving the symptoms, making the child diagnosis-free. Many children and teens will be cured of the disorder. Others, while they will continue to meet the criteria, will benefit from improved symptoms as a result of treatment (therapy, medication). Sometimes the OCD will come and go, and the child will have periods in which she has symptoms that resolve from treatment and then a year later may have another bout of it. It used to be thought that OCD was a lifetime diagnosis, with the person being able to improve but continually at risk of developing symptoms again. Now we know that OCD can be cured, and many children and teens who receive effective treatment will never have OCD again. The research on neuroplasticity shows that the brain can be structurally changed from experience and learning, both of which are accomplished through behavioral change from E/RP. It is important to be committed to the E/RP and believe in your child's ability to overcome the OCD.

A common experience with anxiety and OCD is symptoms that change over time. For example, a child who had the contamination type and resolved those symptoms may then have another theme, such as "just feels right" type, pop up, all during the treatment period. It is best to not be surprised by changing symptoms and instead rely on the treatment process and apply the same strategies to those new

 DOI: 10.4324/9781003237044-9

symptoms. Even in situations when the child overcomes OCD and then it reappears with a new focus and new theme, the same treatment approach applies. That is one of the advantages of CBT: Once you have the skill set, it can be used at any point in the future as well.

Once your child overcomes the OCD, the biggest goal is relapse prevention. The final few sessions I have with a client are on this most important topic. There are three components to it:

1. Continuing to review the techniques from time to time (about 1–2 times a month, going through the folder and reading everything)
2. Continuing to do extended exposure to what should now be reasonably comfortable behavior for your child at this point (for example, eating a sandwich after playing outside in the dirt without washing hands first)
3. Stress management (to be covered in the next chapter)

The reason it is important to review the techniques is, in part, to stay familiar with them so the child can use them as needed, but also to illuminate for the child if there is any return in symptoms that needs to be addressed. For example, one child I saw would regularly read her self-talk cards after she was done with therapy; she and I kept in touch by phone for several months after. During one of these conversations, she said that it was from reading her self-talk cards that she realized there were a "few sticky spots" (symptoms that returned). By reading cards and seeing some that applied to her returning symptoms, the child was able to realize the symptoms were present. This allowed her to be more purposeful and intentional in addressing those symptoms.

The importance of continuing to do exposures cannot be overstated. Think about it like taking baby aspirin after a heart attack: The baby aspirin is used to prevent a known risk from becoming a disease. One aspect of the exposure should be normal for your child because it represents the progress that was made and your child's ability to now, for example, be exposed to germs without washing his hands. So the child who couldn't touch doorknobs who now touches all doorknobs without a tissue or without wearing gloves is in some fashion practicing exposures (it's just that by now they are not supposed to feel like exposures anymore). The other aspect is more reflective of the spirit of the treatment of facing one's fears in an exaggerated, extreme way. Rather than just touching doorknobs like everyone, your child continues to practice touching 10 different doorknobs in 10 minutes and then eating a handful of blueberries. This kind of intentional exposure should be done several times a month in the beginning and then at least once a month moving forward. This is your family's best defense against relapse. And even for the families who do this and still have some relapse, the "round 2" treatment is so much shorter because he was never that out of practice with doing the exposures—it was still fresh for the child. When there is a "round 2" treatment, I typically make a "mini-ladder" on a sheet of paper as opposed to a poster board; I want it to feel less daunting. Typically, the mini-ladder has 4–6 items on it, and often these are new items reflecting new symptoms that have developed. We may also make new worry recordings as well. Again, this will all feel familiar and naturally easier to do in the event that a second course of therapy is needed.

As your child's parent, when you master the best approach to support your child in overcoming her OCD, you become an instrumental part of long-term success in maintaining her progress. You actually become a part of the relapse prevention plan! In a way, you are the best observer of your child's OCD behavior, and if, or when, you notice any symptoms come up, you can point them out. Although your child will likely be aware as well, sometimes she may be doing the behavior automatically and not as tuned in as it would appear. It is important to not hold back in pointing it out, or asking your child directly about the behavior, as there is a lot, be said for "nipping it in the bud." I remember when I was in graduate school and went to an Alcoholics Anonymous (AA) meeting as part of my education on addiction. In that meeting, one of the recovering alcoholics gave a speech on his experience with relapse; he said, "It's the first drink that gets me drunk," meaning that once he has one drink, 10 more will follow. Although it's really the 11th drink that leads to intoxication, it all starts with the first one, which the addict follows with many more. In a way, OCD is similar to addiction: Once the person engages in (even minimal) OCD behavior, it lends itself to more. For the child with OCD, we might say: "It's the first tissue over the doorknob that gets me completely stuck in the cycle." To conclude this point, if you see even a slight gesture that may represent your child engaging in OCD behavior, speak up then and make a goal to work on it at that point—don't wait until it gets worse. It's always easier to treat when it's not that bad, particularly after a successful course of treatment. The key to preventing full-blown relapse is for your child to face any fears that may arise in the future.

Another component of relapse prevention is encouraging your child's confidence in dealing with OCD in the future. Sometimes, a child who overcomes OCD will worry about future bouts of it; in this case, normalize this fear for your child, but assure her that she can overcome it again if necessary. Let her know that if it should come back, treatment the second time is much shorter and easier. You cannot undo the power of success; use it as a confidence-booster for your child. Celebrating your child's treatment success is essential. I always have a celebration at the end and give a mini trophy to symbolize a child's hard work and success. The fear of future OCD doesn't need to be a fear, as there is a formula for treating it and beating it. Build your child's confidence in herself by highlighting what she has been able to do, and explain that those skills are there for her forever. Also, explain that by doing ongoing exposures, she will protect herself against relapse.

It is important that as parents, you make the home environment immune to relapse. Part of this is accomplished by what I said above in terms of recognizing signs of relapse. The other component is making sure the environment naturally encourages exposure. For the child with contamination-type OCD, you want to make sure that things can get dirty and messy and sticky at times; you want to "run out" of hand soap for a day or two, and leave a stain on the carpet for several days before cleaning it. Essentially, you want to give yourself permission to permit some germs and dirt hanging around the house to send a message to the OCD: "We are not afraid of you, OCD! Look at us; we are not keeping this house pristine! You don't live here anymore, and we can do what we want!" It may sound silly to have this dialogue with OCD; however, it is consistent with the frame your child took to overcome it (talking back to the OCD is always encouraged). For the child with perfectionism, make sure things are occasionally out of order, or forgotten about, or that small mistakes happen on a regular basis. With this intention, the message to your child is clear: "We are not organized by OCD anymore. We are free from it!"

A common question I receive is "When is it appropriate to go off the medication?" Although I defer to the prescribing physician (typically a psychiatrist), my general guideline is that once a child has been symptom-free for about 6 months, he can start to wean off the medication. In most cases, the child is able to discontinue the medication without any return of symptoms or side effects. Occasionally, symptoms will return, and if they do, the goal is to treat these symptoms just as we had in the past with the goal of getting rid of them. Most often, the child doesn't need to go back on the medication; rather, he has to return to the hard work of the E/RP and other strategies. A small percentage of children will have too many symptoms (usually intrusive thoughts, not typically a return of the rituals) and will need to either increase back to their full dose, or if they went off completely, increase to a smaller dose. Some children will need to be on medication for several years, but I always recommend a trial to go off of it periodically, as sometimes after puberty they will find that they can be fine without it. The stronger the family history, the more likely that medication will be needed on a longer basis. When you find a medication that works, you want to be grateful for the improvement rather than feel badly about your child being on medication.

As I will discuss in the next chapter, there is some indication that parental anxiety management (PAM), including for nonanxious parents, is beneficial for the long-term treatment outcomes for children with anxiety who receive CBT. Therefore, it is useful for parents to learn how to manage anxiety. PAM, which is about four sessions long, can help parents understand their own anxiety responses and also to gain awareness of what their role can be in helping their child's anxiety challenges. It is my hope that this book, with all of the detailed explanations of CBT treatment for OCD, and ideal parental responses, will be sufficient to have this same positive outcome. On that note, I recommend that you, as the parent, practice the calm breathing, use your own self-talk when stressed or anxious, and find a regular relaxation practice, whether that is yoga or listening to an app. These practices are beneficial for anyone, whether you have a child with OCD or not.

The silver lining of overcoming OCD is that it allows your child to discover his strength and resilience. Although we would prefer to not have obstacles, it's the obstacles in life that cause us to grow and develop. This should be explicitly stated to your child. Let him know that OCD has not been fun, but has made him stronger. It puts your child to the test, and when he overcomes OCD, he will have learned more about himself than he could have imagined. Sometimes a child needs to dig deep to persevere through the natural resistance to the work involved, to find the inner strength to tolerate anxiety and its discomfort, and to trust in a process and in a therapist even before there is good reason to do so. When a child does this, not only is she rewarded by the freedom that comes from overcoming OCD, but she also learns about her strength and her resilience. This is a pretty amazing awareness to develop in one's childhood years. As previously stated, resilience is not letting obstacles stand in our way and knowing that no matter what comes our way, we can handle it. Remind your child of her ability to tolerate discomfort and navigate obstacles, and how this is what resilience is all about. I often see kids show increased confidence in other areas of life after they've successfully navigated through OCD; when you have OCD to compare other obstacles to, the obstacles are often seen as much smaller and more conquerable. This shift in perspective also fuels the resilience.

Finally, it is a fact that stress worsens OCD and also increases the chance of relapse. When your child is stressed, he must use strategies to manage it well. Although this is true for all children (and adults), it is particularly important for someone who has OCD because stress poses a risk for relapse. The next chapter is on stress management, which should not only be an integral part of your child's treatment, but also a necessary ongoing measure that ensures continued progress.

Chapter 9

Stress Management

Managing stress is an important part of living a healthy, rewarding life. Achieving a good balance between (school) work and life and learning how to have downtime and enjoy life are essential for one's well-being. For children and teens with OCD, managing stress is not only a part of their overall health, but also a necessary component of overcoming OCD and maintaining progress in the years to come.

Children and teens with OCD consistently report that their symptoms worsen at times of stress. When they are stressed, they are more symptomatic and have a harder time fighting the OCD. Sometimes to relieve their stress, they give in more easily to the OCD because it provides a sense of quick relief (although, of course, it makes OCD worse for them in the long run). Stress can be experienced as intermittent (for example, an upcoming exam or disagreement with a friend) or chronic (for example, being overwhelmed by daily homework and responsibilities or being in a home where there is a lot of arguing/screaming). As much as possible, we want the home environment to be predictable, consistent, and as calm as possible.

When we think of managing stress, there are four basics that you want to emphasize with your child:

1. sleeping well
2. eating well
3. exercising
4. relaxation and meditation

 DOI: 10.4324/9781003237044-10

The Importance of Sleep

Let's start with the first basic: sleep. When it comes to sleeping well, this means quality and quantity. For most children and teens, a bedtime routine and good sleep hygiene will create good quality sleep. Sleep hygiene involves the following: going to bed and waking up around the same time every night (within an hour on each end), not eating or drinking at least an hour before bed, not using screens within 45 minutes of bed, and not doing anything other than sleeping in one's bed (no homework, texting, watching TV, etc. from bed) so that bed is associated only with sleep. If it takes more than 20 minutes and your child is not asleep, he should get out of bed and do something relatively mundane until he feels sleepy and then can return to bed. However, children can listen to a relaxation CD or app from bed. Most children and teens need 8–10 hours of sleep a night, although most teens get much less. Children who have too little sleep and a lot of stress can end up with adrenal fatigue and feel tired all the time. When this is the case, adrenal and immune support are imperative. Talk with your pediatrician or alternative doctors to learn more about what can be done to combat adrenal fatigue and boost the immune system, such as improving eating habits.

The Importance of a Healthy Diet

Eating well involves eating mostly whole foods (the food itself is the ingredient, such as an apple, which is just an apple), vegetables, fruit, legumes, and lean protein such as organic and pasture-raised eggs and grass-fed meat. Organic foods are preferable, as they do not have pesticides, hormones, or antibiotics in them. Certainly, you want to avoid eating any processed foods or foods with high fructose corn syrup, partially hydrogenated oils, and "isolated" anything (e.g., soy protein isolate) as much as possible. Switching from soda to water or seltzer water can do wonders for one's health, and it is important to drink a lot of purified water. Chronic stress leads to inflammation, which can create oxidative stress and therefore free radicals that cause disease in the body. Adopting an anti-inflammatory diet is an excellent way to counter the impact of stress from anxiety and OCD. And this should be a family's agenda, not just for the individual with OCD. Antioxidants such as berries, broccoli, asparagus, and dark green leafy vegetables (kale, spinach, Swiss chard) should be incorporated into the daily diet. Flax seed (ground), turmeric, ginger root, and dandelion root all have anti-inflammatory properties. All of these foods can be gradually introduced into your child's diet. Always introduce new foods in combination with familiar foods and be persistent in integrating these foods. Magnesium has been show to help with anxiety and stress (it can be taken in pill or powder form); ask your pediatrician for dosing information. Finally, the supplement NAC (N-Acetyl Cysteine), which is a glutamate modulator, is showing good promise in the treatment of OCD (Oliver et al., 2015). Essentially, managing stress includes nutrition and possible supplements to help counter the impact of stress on the body.

The Importance of Exercise

Exercise has consistently been proven to help with stress, anxiety, and mood regulation. Too many of us are sedentary, and we need to move; this includes children and teens who often spend time on screens. When kids I've worked with begin exercising or doing yoga, they report an improved ability to manage their anxiety. Encourage your child to stay active and be creative in suggesting activities that are naturally fun but also involve movement. Once it becomes part of one's routine, it is easy and rewarding.

The Importance of
Relaxation and Meditation

Practicing relaxation and possibly learning meditation will enhance your child's life (and hopefully yours, too). Even 10 minutes of listening to a relaxation app before bedtime will help (see the Resources section for a list of great apps). We cannot underestimate the power of the mind-body connection; when you relax the body, the mind can let go, and when you calm the mind, the body calms, too. Being in nature supports mental health and can be a very relaxing and grounding experience for children and teens. In Richard Louv's 2005 book *Last Child in the Woods,* it is explained that children are spending too little time in nature, and their mental/emotional (including self-confidence), physical, and spiritual health is compromised as a result. Being in nature encourages more creativity and intelligence. It also allows a child to get out of her head, away from thoughts, and in connection with her surroundings. Part of managing stress is ensuring enough time outdoors.

Additional Recommendations

In addition, you want to encourage your child to express and talk about his feelings and what is causing him stress, so he is not holding onto anything or keeping anything in. Sometimes simply venting or listing out all of his stressors or worry situations is sufficient to help him feel better. It is also important to try to prevent stress from building up. For example, staying on top of schoolwork and creating a schedule that reflects a good balance between work and pleasure are ideal. Help your child create a realistic schedule in which she is not overcommitting, is leaving extra time to complete tasks, and has some time off to truly unwind (we are not designed to go-go-go). Finally, creating a good relationship with technology and technology use is now forevermore an important piece of stress management. I also recommend avoiding the news as much as possible; news is one of the best examples of the selective attention thinking error, and in my experience, few people feel calm and at peace after watching all of the bad things that have happened in the world!

Children are growing up in a screen-filled society where an abundance of information is literally at their fingertips 24/7. The energy of screens, filled with ongoing motion and sometimes commotion, must be mitigated with things like the energy of nature, meditation, and exercise. Social media could even be a trigger for teens with OCD. I have had many cases where the obsessive-compulsive behavior was targeted on social media: looking at someone's photos over and over and triggering social comparisons, FOMO (fear of missing out), and many thinking errors (selective attention being the most common) that cause anxiety. Parents need to establish limits with screens and ensure that children are balancing time on social media with time on other (arguably more rewarding) pursuits. Having "screen breaks" and "social media vacations" is highly recommended. The goal is *not* to live without technology or social media; the goal is to establish a healthy relationship with it, and parents should provide a good model for this, just as they should provide a good model for stress management in general. Eating meals with no screens at the table, for example, is a great value for families to model.

Stress management for your child's OCD does not just apply to him. Being a parent of a child with OCD can be exhausting and depleting; doing the accommodations creates a great deal of stress. As stated, families who engage in accommodations have higher stress levels. Parents need their own stress management plan, whether it's taking 15 minutes before bed to meditate or listening to a meditation on an app (such as Insight Timer), exercising every other day, or going to a support group for parents of kids with OCD or anxiety. Your stress level will affect your child: If you are stressed, he will feel it and will likely be stressed as well. It is not surprising to learn that untreated parental anxiety interferes with the successfulness of child-focused CBT for anxiety (Cobham, Dadds, Spence, & McDermott, 2010; Kendall, Hudson, Gosch, Flannery-Schroeder, & Suveg, 2008; Rapee, Schniering, & Hudson, 2009). Parental anxiety management (PAM), in which parents (whether they had their own anxiety or not) received training to manage their own anxiety and clarify their role in helping their child, has been associated with greater improvement in anxious children who had received CBT treatment; these children also had a higher chance of being anxiety-free at 3-year follow-up periods (Cobham et al., 2010). The point is that if you have your own anxiety, it should be treated, and if you don't but you have a child with anxiety, your child will benefit if you learn about anxiety management and your role in his difficulties.

In summary, successful treatment of OCD includes relapse prevention and stress management, and these are not tasks for your child to manage on his own; rather, it is part of the family system's goal in promoting and maintaining wellness. In this way, the silver lining of OCD, in addition to promoting self-awareness and resilience, can be to achieve a greater level of well-being.

Finally, I strongly believe in you and your child's ability to overcome OCD. I have witnessed the success of CBT for OCD time and time again. With the right help, this enormous obstacle will become little more than a short detour. I wish you and your family all the best throughout the treatment process.

Resources

Recommended Books for Parents and Professionals

General Anxiety

Bourne, E. J. (2015). *The anxiety & phobia workbook* (6th ed.). Oakland, CA: New Harbinger.

Leahy, R. L. (2006). *The worry cure: Seven steps to stop worry from stopping you.* New York, NY: Harmony Books.

Wilson, R., & Lyons, L. (2013). *Anxious kids, anxious parents: 7 ways to stop the worry cycle and raise courageous and independent children.* Deerfield Beach, FL: HCI Publishing.

Zucker, B. (2017). *Anxiety-free kids: An interactive guide for parents and children* (2nd ed.). Waco, TX: Prufrock Press.

Social Anxiety

Antony, M. M., & Swinson, R. P. (2008). *The shyness and social anxiety workbook: Proven step-by-step techniques for overcoming your fear* (2nd ed.). Oakland, CA: New Harbinger.

Panic Attacks

Wilson, R. R. (2003). *Facing panic: Self-help for people with panic attacks.* Silver Spring, MD: Anxiety Disorders Association of America.

Perfectionism

Adelson, J. L., & Wilson, H. E. (2009). *Letting go of perfect: Overcoming perfectionism in kids.* Waco, TX: Prufrock Press.

Antony, M. M., & Swinson, R. P. (2009). *When perfect isn't good enough: Strategies for coping with perfectionism* (2nd ed.). Oakland, CA: New Harbinger.

Braiker, H. B. (2002). *The disease to please: Curing the people-pleasing syndrome.* New York, NY: McGraw-Hill.

Health Anxiety

Taylor, S., & Asmundson, G. J. G. (2004). *Treating health anxiety: A cognitive-behavioral approach.* New York, NY: Guilford Press.

Hair Pulling

Keuthen, N. J., Stein, D. J., & Christenson, G. A. (2001). *Help for hair pullers: Understanding and coping with trichotillomania.* Oakland, CA: New Harbinger.

Mouton-Odum, S., & Golomb, R. G. (2013). *A parent guide to hair pulling disorder: Effective parenting strategies for children with trichotillomania.* Washington, DC: Goldum Publishing.

Penzel, F. (2003). *The hair-pulling problem: A complete guide to trichotillomania.* New York, NY: Oxford University Press.

Medication

Wilens, T. E., & Hammerness, P. G. (2016). *Straight talk about psychiatric medications for kids* (4th ed.). New York, NY: Guilford Press.

Mindfulness and Meditation and Yoga

NurrieStearns, M., & NurrieStearns, R. (2010). *Yoga for anxiety: Meditations and practices for calming the body and mind.* Oakland, CA: New Harbinger.

Singer, M.A. (2007). *The untethered soul: The journey beyond yourself.* Oakland, CA: New Harbinger.

Recommended Books for Children

Covey, S. (2014). *The 7 habits of highly effective teens.* New York, NY: Touchstone.

Flanagan, E. (2014). *Ten turtles on Tuesday: A story for children about obsessive-compulsive disorder.* Washington, DC: Magination Press.

Golomb, R. G., & Vavrichek, S. M. (2000). *The hair pulling "habit" and you: How to solve the trichotillomania puzzle* (Rev. ed.). Silver Spring, MD: Writers Cooperative of Greater Washington.

Guber, T., & Kalish, L. (2005). *Yoga pretzels.* Cambridge, MA: Barefoot Books. (Yoga cards)

Huebner, D. (2007). *What to do when your brain gets stuck: A kid's guide to overcoming OCD.* Washington, DC: Magination Press.

Wagner, A. P., & Jutton, P. A. (2013). *Up and down the worry hill: A children's book about obsessive-compulsive disorder and its treatment.* Rochester, NY: Lighthouse Press.

Zucker, B. (2011). *Take control of OCD: The ultimate guide for kids with OCD.* Waco, TX: Prufrock Press.

Recommended CDs

Alvord, M., Zucker, B., & Alvord, B. (2011). *Relaxation and self-regulation techniques for children and teens: Mastering the mind-body connection* [Audio CD]. Champaign, IL: Research Press.

Charlesworth, E. A. (2002). *Scanning relaxation* [Audio CD]. Champaign, IL: Research Press.

Lite, L. (2006). *Indigo dreams: Relaxation and stress management bedtime stories for children, improve sleep, manage stress and anxiety* [Audio CD]. Marietta, GA: Lite Books.

Recommended Apps

Calm (http://calm.com)
CBT Tools for Youth
Headspace
Insight Timer
iSleep Easy

Organizations

American Psychological Association (APA)
750 First Street, NE
Washington, DC 20002
800-374-2721
http://www.apa.org
http://www.apa.org/helpcenter

The Anxiety and Depression Association of America (ADAA)
8701 Georgia Avenue, Suite 412
Silver Spring, MD 20910
240-485-1001
http://www.adaa.org

Association for Behavioral and Cognitive Therapies (ABCT)
305 7th Avenue, 16th Fl.
New York, NY 10001
212-647-1890
http://www.abct.org

The Child Anxiety Network
http://www.childanxiety.net

International OCD Foundation (IOCDF)
P.O. Box 961029
Boston, MA 02196
617-973-5801
http://www.iocdf.org

National Alliance on Mental Illness (NAMI)
3803 N. Fairfax Drive, Suite 100
Arlington, VA 22203
800-950-6264
http://www.nami.org

National Institute of Mental Health (NIMH)
Science Writing, Press, and Dissemination Branch
6001 Executive Boulevard, Room 6200, MSC 9663
Bethesda, MD 20892
866-615-6464
http://www.nimh.nih.gov

The TLC Foundation for Body-Focused Repetitive Behaviors
716 Soquel Ave., Suite A
Santa Cruz, CA 95062
831-457-1004
http://www.bfrb.org

Inpatient and Day Treatment Programs Specifically for OCD

This list is not exhaustive; for a larger list, visit http://www.iocdf.

The Gateway Institute (Arizona; also in California)
9375 E Shea Blvd, Ste. 100
Scottsdale, AZ 85260
(800) 223-6148
http://www.gatewayocd.com

Houston OCD Program
708 E. 19th Street
Houston, TX 77008
(713) 526-5055
http://www.houstonocdprogram.org

Intensive Treatment Program for OCD and Anxiety
at Weill Cornell Medicine
1300 York Avenue
New York, NY 10065
(646) 962-2820
http://www.weillcornellpsychiatrycenter.org

The Lindner Center of HOPE:
OC and Anxiety Disorder Treatment Programs
4075 Old Western Row Rd.
Mason, OH 45040
(513) 536-4673
http://www.lindnercenterofhope.org

Louisville OCD Clinic
912 Lily Creek Rd, Ste. 201
Louisville, KY 40243
(502) 403-7818
http://www.louisvilleocdclinic.com

McLean Hospital OCD Institute
115 Mill Street
Belmont, MA 02478
(800) 333-0338
http://www.mcleanhospital.org

Mount Sinai Obsessive-Compulsive and Related Disorders Program
1425 Madison Avenue
Department of Psychiatry, 4th Floor
New York, NY 10029
(212) 659-8823
http://www.mountsinaiocd.org

OCD & Anxiety Program of Southern California
2656 29th Street, Ste. 208
Santa Monica, CA 90405
(310) 488-5850
http://www.socalocdprogram.org

The OCD and Anxiety Treatment Center
1459 North Main Street
Bountiful, UT 84010
(801) 298-2000
http://www.theocdandanxietytreatmentcenter.com

The OCD Clinics (multiple locations in Texas)
262 N. Union Street
New Braunfels, TX 78130
(830) 237-5724
http://www.theocdclinics.com

Pediatric Psychology Associates' Anxiety and OCD Intensive
Outpatient Program (Aventura)
2925 Aventura Blvd., Ste. 300
Aventura, FL 33180
(305) 936-1002
http://www.southfloridatherapists.com

Potomac Behavioral Solutions
2001 Jefferson Davis Highway, Ste. 211
Arlington, VA 22202
(571) 257-3378
http://www.pbshealthcare.com

Psychological Care & Healing (PCH) OCD Intensive Treatment
Program
11965 Venice Blvd, Ste. 202
Los Angeles, CA 90066
(888) 724-0040
http://www.pchtreatment.com

Rogers Behavioral Health OCD Center (multiple locations)
34700 Valley Rd.
Oconomowoc, WI 53066
(800) 767-4411
http://www.rogersbh.org

UCLA Child & Adolescent OCD Intensive Outpatient Treatment
Program
Semel Institute
760 Westwood Plaza, 67-467
Los Angeles, CA 90024
(310) 825-0122
http://www.semel.ucla.edu/caap/ocd-intensive-treatment

References

Albert, U., Bogetto, F., Maina, G., Saracco, P., Brunatto, C., & Mataix-Cols, D. (2010). Family accommodation in obsessive-compulsive disorder: Relation to symptom dimensions, clinical and family characteristics. *Psychiatry Research, 179,* 204–211.

American Psychiatric Association. (2013). *Diagnostic and statistical manual of mental disorders* (5th ed.). Washington, DC: Author.

Amir, N., Freshman, M., & Foa, E. (2000). Family distress and involvement in relatives of obsessive-compulsive disorder patients. *Journal of Anxiety Disorders, 14,* 209–217.

Barlow, D. (2004). Psychological treatments. *American Psychologist, 59,* 869–878.

Baumrind, D. (1971). Current patterns of parental authority. *Developmental Psychology Monograph, 4,* (1, Pt. 2).

Benito, K., & Freeman, J. B. (2011). Pediatric anxiety: How family accommodation may hinder treatment. *Brown University Child and Adolescent Behavior Letter, 27*(3).

Boileau, B. (2011). A review of obsessive-compulsive disorder in children and adolescents. *Dialogues in Clinical Neuroscience, 13,* 401–411.

Ciarrocchi, J. W. (1995). *The doubting disease: Help for scrupulosity and religious compulsions.* New York, NY: Integration Books.

Cobham, V. E., Dadds, M. R., Spence, S. H., & McDermott, B. (2010). Parental anxiety in the treatment of childhood anxiety: A different story three years later. *Journal of Clinical Child & Adolescent Psychology, 39,* 410–420.

Covey, S. (2014). *The 7 habits of highly effective teens.* New York, NY: Simon & Schuster.

Erikson, E. H. (1963). *Childhood and society* (2nd ed.). New York, NY: Norton.

Ferrao, Y. A., Shavitt, R. G., Bedin, N. R., de Mathis, M. E., Lopes, C. A., Fontenelle, L. F., . . . Miguel, E. C. (2006). Clinical features associated to refractory obsessive-compulsive disorder. *Journal of Affective Disorders, 94,* 199–209.

Greist, J., & Baudhuin, M. (n.d.). *What you need to know about obsessive compulsive disorder.* Retrieved from https://iocdf.org/wp-content/uploads/2014/10/What-You-Need-To-Know-About-OCD.pdf

Harris, R. (2009). *ACT made simple: An easy-to-read primer on acceptance and commitment therapy.* Oakland, CA: New Harbinger.

Hollon, S. D., Stewart, M. O., & Strunk, D. (2006). Enduring effects for cognitive behavior therapy in the treatment of depression and anxiety. *Annual Review of Psychology, 57,* 285–315.

Hyman, B. M., & Pedrick, C. (2010). *The OCD workbook: Your guide to breaking free from obsessive-compulsive disorder* (3rd ed.). Oakland, CA: New Harbinger.

Kendall, P. C., Hudson, J. L., Gosch, E., Flannery-Schroeder, E., & Suveg, C. (2008). Cognitive-behavioral therapy for anxiety disordered youth: A randomized clinical trial evaluating child and family modalities. *Journal of Consulting and Clinical Psychology, 76,* 282–297.

Leahy, R. L. (2006). *The worry cure: Seven steps to stop worry from stopping you.* New York, NY: Harmony Books.

Lebowitz, E. R., Panza, K. E., Su, J., & Bloch, M. H. (2012). Family accommodation in obsessive-compulsive disorder. *Expert Review of Neurotherapeutics, 12,* 229–38.

Louv, R. (2005). *Last child in the woods: Saving our children from nature-deficit disorder.* Chapel Hill, NC: Algonquin Books.

Oliver, G., Dean, O., Camfield, D., Blair-West, S., Ng, C., Berk, M., & Sarris, J. (2015). N-Acetyl Cysteine in the treatment of obsessive compulsive and related disorders: A systematic review. *Clinical Psychopharmacology and Neuroscience, 13,* 12–24.

Rapee, R. M., Schniering, C. A., & Hudson, J. L. (2009). Anxiety disorders during childhood and adolescence: Origins and treatment. *Annual Review of Clinical Psychology, 5,* 311–341.

Rosen, M., & Oxenbury, H. (1997). *We're going on a bear hunt.* New York, NY: Little Simon.

Ruscio, A. M., Stein, D. J., Chiu, W. T., & Kessler, R. C. (2010). The epidemiology of obsessive-compulsive disorder in the National Comorbidity Survey Replication. *Journal of Molecular Psychiatry, 15,* 53–63.

Storch, E. A., Geffken, G. R., Merlo, L. J., Jacob, M. L., Murphy, T. K., Goodman, W. K., . . . Grabill, K. (2007). Family accommodation in pediatric obsessive-compulsive disorder. *Journal of Clinical Child & Adolescent Psychology, 36,* 207–216.

Walkup, J. T., Albano, A. M., Piacentini, J., Birmaher, B., Compton, S. N., Sherrill, J. T., . . . Kendall, P. C. (2008). Cognitive behavioral therapy, sertraline, or a combination in childhood anxiety. *New England Journal of Medicine, 359,* 2753–2766.

Wells, A. (2011). *Metacognitive therapy for anxiety and depression.* New York, NY: Guilford Press.

About the Author

Bonnie Zucker, Psy.D., is a licensed psychologist with a background and expertise in psychotherapy with children, adolescents, and adults. She received her doctoral degree in clinical psychology from Illinois School of Professional Psychology in Chicago, her master's degree in applied psychology from University of Baltimore, and her bachelor's degree in psychology from The George Washington University.

Dr. Zucker specializes in the treatment of childhood anxiety disorders and OCD. Using a cognitive-behavioral (CBT) approach, she has helped children overcome their OCD by teaching them coping skills, methods for challenging their faulty thinking, and doing Exposure/Response Prevention (E/RP). Dr. Zucker also works with parents to guide them in how to best respond to their child's OCD.

Dr. Zucker is in private practice in Rockville, MD. She was named one of *Washingtonian* Magazine's Top Therapists in several fields, including CBT, OCD, and Phobias. In addition to being active in training mental health professionals on the treatment of anxiety disorders and OCD, Dr. Zucker wrote *Anxiety-Free Kids: An Integrative Guide for Parents and Children* (now in its second edition), *Take Control of OCD: The Ultimate Guide for Kids With OCD*, and *Something Very Sad Happened: A Toddler's Guide to Understanding Death*. She also coauthored *Resilience Builder Program for Children and Adolescents: Enhancing Social Competence and Self-Regulation (A Cognitive-Behavioral Group Approach)*, *Relaxation and Self-Regulation Techniques for Children and Teens: Mastering the Mind-Body Connection* (Audio CD), and *Relaxation and Wellness Techniques: Mastering the Mind-Body Connection* (Audio CD).